GERALD
MONSMAN

AF608891

JOHN TREVENA

HIS WEST COUNTRY NOVELS

UNIVERSITY PRESS
OF THE SOUTH

2021

Copyright 2021 by Gerald Monsman.

All rights reserved. No part of this publication may be reproduced, stored in a retrieval system, or transmitted, in any form or by any means, electronic, mechanical, photocopying, recording or otherwise, without the prior written permission of the Publisher.
Published in the United States by The University Press of the South. Printed in France by Monbeaulivre.fr

E-mails: unprsouth@aol.com ; universitypresssouth@gmail.com
Visit our award-winning web pages: www.unprsouth.com; www.punouveaumonde.com.

Gerald Monsman.

John Trevena: His West Country Novels.

Second Edition in English.

viii + 168 pages. British and Irish Studies, 12.

Front Cover Art: 'John Trevena Writing at his Desk ca. 1912.'

Reproduced with permission.

1. Trevena, John. 2. Henham, Ernest G. 3. 19th Century English Biography. 4. 20th century English Biography. 5. Parapsychology. 6. Dartmoor (England). 7. Landscape in Literature. 8. Myth in Literature. 9. Nature in Literature. 10. Religion in literature.

ISBN: 978-1-937030-32-2 (USA Edition, 2013)
ISBN: 978-1-952799-41-9 (European Edition, 2021)

This one

is for

AN

An Monsman
Dartmoor Forest Rocks

"All your pictures are silent poems."

Unknown Ancient Roman Author.

JOHN TREVENA: HIS WEST COUNTRY NOVELS

TABLE OF CONTENTS

PREFACE

Ernest George Henham (1870–1948), writing both under his own name and with the pseudonym of "John Trevena," has until now been a "lost" writer, yet of remarkable achievement; indeed, he is a writer of greater range and power than any other West Country author with the possible exception of the more celebrated Thomas Hardy–who remains very much in print. Nevertheless, Henham/ Trevena also is surely a masterfulEnglish language novelist and a cultural figure of courage and vision, responding to social, political, and religious change with insight and contestation. I say it with reluctance–and I say this despite the marvelous additions brought to the literary canon by feminist and minority studies specialists–but with the exception of new women writers or writers belonging to specific cultural groups, our academic media during my career have been reluctant to swerve more than two or three points to the right or left of figures that have caught the eye of the intellectual *fashionistas*. But the literary canon is potentially more fluid than our readership assumes, and the consensus that rules the period of English literature in transition (1880–1920) should be open to greater debate than it is. Of course, simple newness can be mere faddishness and shaky claims of novelty may drive out firmer ones, but this should not promote canon-induced rigor mortis.

As the first book-length monograph on Henham/Trevena in eighty years, *John Trevena: His West Country Novels* focuses in particular on his Dartmoor fiction and its connection to his personal life. Given his prolific output of some twenty-seven novels–as well as a volume on wild flowers and numerous short stories and essays–this critique does not pretend to be exhaustively inclusive. Its purpose is to reintroduce his writings to renewed critical consideration, and its method is selective discussion of his best Dartmoor fiction. It will combine the original response to his novels with new biographical facts that bolster insight into his authorial intent, applying a methodology that puts the Dartmoor sceneswithin the context of wider literary, historical, and political-social developments. While early twentieth-century reviewers tended a bit more than current ones to take to heart Thumper's father's advice that "if you can't say something nice, don't say nothing at all," their opinions of Henham/Trevena are anything but faint praise. Indeed, one impetus for extending this study to book-length was my desire to understand how such world-class evaluations could belong to a writer who appears to merit only footnote status in the most exhaustive surveys of English literature.

After situating his works within their literary period, the next two chapters are devoted to his life and bifurcated career as Henham/Trevena, including discussion of one novel from among his earlier fiction. (And since this is the first attempt to write a critical biography, for the sake of further investigation some primary source documentation is supplied here at greater length than may be customary.) The chapters following will undertake a chronological analysis of eight novels between 1906 and 1913 in which the focus will be: first, on his fiction's reception and the biographical issues of his literary craft; second, on the narrative patterns and ideational content of his works in the very widest possible sense of Aristotle's *mythos*–the specific incidents and the author's rendering of motives and effects. Trevena is a complexly subtle thinker and these "readings" of his fiction are preliminary and by no means all-inclusive–exploratory"sallies of the mind" in a quest for an understanding that is ongoing.

Undertaken originally as the "2011 Lectures" for the History of Ideas Institute, this series is now brought to publication by the Institute's generous support. I am pleased also to be able to thank cordially Jay Jenkins of Valancourt Books and Roger Brean of the Devon and Exeter Institution Library, Exeter, for their support. For brevity, parenthetical page-number-only citations refer back either to the name or title in the text or to a preceding parenthetical citation.

CHAPTER 1

THE CASE FOR TREVENA

One of the pleasures for readers of late-Victorian and Edwardian novels is the abundance of neglected texts to be discovered–that, and the opportunity of reintroducing their forgotten authors to a wider critical discourse. Varying social and political contexts produce differing constructions of value and those which one era embraces, the next to its imaginative impoverishment may ignore. One thinks of the droll response of T. E. Brown, the regional Manx poet, upon being told late in life by a sympathetic friend that he "had been omitted from a list of minor writers of the Victorian period. Brown smiled and said, 'Perhaps I am among the major'" (Tobias 12). On the Isle of Man there would be no irony or wistfulness found in this riposte. But elsewhere the relentless pursuit of the currently fashionable has left Brown, like John Trevena, ignored. A leap of the historical imagination is required to hark back to Trevena's early twentieth-century preoccupations, to appreciate his fierce humanitarianism, his iconoclasm in religious feelings, his sense of nature's beauty and cruelty, and his poetic response to life's tragedies. Trevena's novels may well be ideal candidates for reclamation. Might they not, if rediscovered, generate a classic richness and diversity of interpretation?

The time is right–ambitious though it may seem–to argue that he deserves to be read alongside his more famous West Country compatriot, Thomas Hardy, although Trevena is the more-recondite writer. Trevena's use of the land as a metaphor of its people, a place of the mind as well as a topography that is real, has an originality all its own. Samuel Dibble asserted that "When it comes to analyzing provincial England with its multiplicity of conflicting characteristics and traits that have come down through centuries of varying civilizations, it is probable Mr. Trevena has no equal" (4). The only previous book-length study of Trevena's work has been an able but limited-circulation dissertation some eighty years ago; however, in the meantime newer interpretive methodologies have been forged, better able to make sense of Trevena if carefully applied. As an opportunity for innovative canon revision, a new study analyzing the artistic handling of his thematic materials will add a new "intellectual novelist" to the canon.

So how–specifically–does one begin to make the case for John Trevena*redivivus*? Essentially, he is a regional novelist whose work, set among the Dartmoor valleys and rocky hilltops, exhibits a strong feel for social customs and realistic dialogue. Not every writer's representation of local life and landscape has appeal and excellence, of course; some are mediocre productions goosed up with over-zealous applications of regional color. The most praiseworthy regional novels, as we currently know them, probably hark back to Maria Edgeworth and Sir Walter Scott. Many other regional works of the nineteenth century, such as those by Elizabeth Gaskell, Charles Kingsley, and the Brontës also belong among the most successful in that genre, as well as Thomas Hardy'sWessex novels that have the closest affinity with Trevena's writings–particularly Hardy's vision of nature's resistless power and cruelties. This regional tradition has remained vital throughout the last century as well–James Joyce, Virginia Woolf, or William Faulkner and his Southern compatriots; not to mention that rapidly growing part of the literary landscape in our twenty-first century, black and ethnic urban writing. What W. B. Yeats defined in "Synge and Ireland" as the Celtic achievement of his Irish countryman's plays may be said of Trevena also: "He loves all that has edge, all that is salt in the mouth, all that is rough to the hand, all that heightens the emotions by contest, all that stings into life the sense of tragedy. . . . Synge, like all of the great kin, sought for the race, not through the eyes or in history, or even in the future, but where those monks found God, in the depths of the mind" (326-327, 341). Such an ethos may be discovered either in rural or urban environments–Trevena's tended to be rural, the folk living amidst the "cleaves" and "tors" of Dartmoor. J. M. Synge's "depths of the mind" or the "inmost consciousness" of the Manx which Brown had taken as his theme–a race that, despite Brown's love of his people, he finds tainted by human fallenness–this also is Trevena's theme.

Thomas Hardy may have provided a preliminary insight into the value of regional fiction when he wrote that novels such as his *Tess of the D'Urbervilles* (1891) were meant to be "a fairly true record of a vanishing life" (Hardy, General Preface). Such cultural "life," Sir Edward Burnett Tylor said, was the "complex whole which includes knowledge, belief, art, morals, law, custom, and any other capabilities and habits acquired by man as a member of society" (1:1). In *Heather* (1908) Trevena wrote:

> The present inhabitants are our subject; the last dregs of the folk, still ignorant and primitive, who are being killed like the Red Indians by the civilisation which has for a long time surrounded and is now breaking over them, driving out the old, bringing in the new, ringing out the age of mettle, of muscle, sinew, and simplicity, and heralding the age of skill, brains, and trickery. Bigbones has finished his reign and must go to the wall against which he has been wont to push Littlebones. Evolution stays for nothing; first vegetation, then reptiles, then mammals, and now brains. The age of cunning has begun; and God help the giant." (29)

Put simply, Trevena's theme is the comedy and tragedy of the Bronze Age confronting modernity. He was sensitive to what today we call a "third space" or a borderland threshold–in this instance an ancient, all-but-independent Duchy confronting trains, electricity, and novel ideologies. Writers living on such temporal and spatial borders have a firsthand opportunity to instruct and enliven by detailing the processes of cultural interchange. As do cultural studies of other human societies, Trevena's fiction emphasizes unique interpersonal and intergroup relations, those antagonisms and connections effectively focused through the passions of love and similar catastrophes.

Behind the human comedy of Trevena's Dartmoor were the Wessex novels of Thomas Hardy–originally controversial, but clearly and deservedly now canonical, integral to an appreciation of England's rural heritage. Yet in depicting the vagaries of humans and nature, Hardy is almost cinematically visual compared with Trevena who utilizes two different descriptive techniques: an intimately psychological presentation of character reflecting the emerging complexities of consciousness in modern fiction (a foreshadowing of Virginia Woolf's "luminous halo, a semi-transparent envelope" of an "unknown and uncircumscribed spirit"[189]) and, offsetting this, a satire of the buffooneries of the Dartmoor rustics, a comedy that looks both back to the eccentric personages of Charles Dickens or the self-satirizing of Charles Lamb in "A Dissertation Upon Roast Pig"–and also, as likely as not, ahead to darker human defects in post-modernism. Pertaining to such eccentrics, Willum and Ann Cobbledick are the starring oddities in *A Pixy in Petticoats* (1906), precursors to Peter and Mary Tavy in Trevena's *Furze the Cruel* (1907). Even so, in terms of these agricultural and village rustics, neither Thomas Hardy's Wessex nor Trevena's Dartmoor presents formalized local color figures, as in a Greek chorus or, sometimes, among Shakespeare's "clowns." Across the repertoire of Trevena's many different sorts of narratives–playful, historical, dramatic, psychological–his authentic figures of broad comedy give zest and ebullience to the narrative, even when edged with horrific or tragic possibilities. *Furze the Cruel* and most of his West Country novels are a kind of ethnography or informal social anthropology emphasizing, like cultural studies of other human societies, unique interpersonal and intergroup relations, the "inmost" social connections.

Hardy's essay "The Dorsetshire Labourer" in *Longman's Magazine* (July, 1883) indicts genteel society for supposing agricultural workers are uniformly alike. "Hodge" was Hardy's personification for the sort of backward rustic laborer that many assumed any West Country visitor would encounter:

> This supposed real but highly conventional Hodge is a degraded being of uncouth manner and aspect, stolid understanding, and snail-like movement. His speech is such a chaotic corruption of regular language that few persons of progressive aims consider it worth while to enquire what views, if any, of life, of nature, or of society, are conveyed in these utterances. . . . But living on there for a few days the sojourner would . . . find that the language, instead of being a vile corruption of cultivated speech, was a tongue with a grammatical inflection rarely disregarded by his entertainer, though his [host's] children would occasionally make a sad hash of their talk. Dick the carter, Bob the shepherd, and Sam the ploughman, are, it is true, alike in the narrowness of their means and their general open-air life; but they cannot be rolled together again into such a Hodge as [the visitor] dreamt of, by any possible enchantment.

Like Hodge, Trevena's characters lived in England's southwest counties, Dorset, Devon, and Cornwall, areas of lower wages, loosely knit social networks, and coldly impersonal interactions between employers and workers. And like Hardy, Trevena insists upon the richness of their personal variations. The identity of both authors' characters typically is rooted in the landscape; they are vivid, unique, tied to place, true to their heritage–although Treven-aseems acutely aware of a lost sea-going glory. Hardy, too, comments on this decline of Dorset from its robust past:

> During the centuries of serfdom, of copyholding tenants, and down to twenty or thirty years ago, before the power of unlimited migration had been clearly realised, the husbandman of either class had the interest of long personal association with his farm. The fields were those he had ploughed and sown from boyhood, and it was impossible for him, in such circumstances, to sink altogether the character of natural guardian in that of hireling. . . . A depopulation is going on which in some quarters is truly alarming. Villages used to contain, in addition to the agricultural inhabitants, an interesting and better-informed class, ranking distinctly above those–the blacksmith, the carpenter, the shoemaker, the small higgler, the shopkeeper (whose stock-in-trade consisted of a couple of loaves, a pound of candles, a bottle of brandy-balls and lumps of delight, three or four scrubbing-brushes, and a frying-pan), together with nondescript-workers other than farm-labourers, who had remained in the houses where they were born for no especial reason beyond an instinct of association with the spot. . . . The occupants who formed the back-bone of the village life have to seek refuge in the boroughs. This process, which is designated by statisticians as "the tendency of the rural population towards the large towns," is really the tendency of water to flow uphill when forced. The poignant regret of those who are thus obliged to forsake the old nest can only be realised by people who have witnessed it–concealed as it often is under a mask of indifference. (252-269)

As a spectator of contemporary Dartmoor life, John Trevena's intention is not merely to describe the "cruel" land or to chronicle its rural poor, but to show how the landscape is formative of the inhabitants' life-traits and souls. Little did Trevena realize, during his early Canadian phase, how close he came to Hardy's expedient use of materials taken from the landscape for writing: Hardy "could meditate on his subject as he walked in congenial surroundings on the heath or in the neighbouring woods, jotting down his thoughts, sometimes, when he had no scrap of paper with him, on 'large dead leaves, white chips left by the wood-cutters, or pieces of stone or slate that came to hand'; he had found that 'when he carried a pocket-book his mind was barren as the Sahara'" (Pinnion 111). Trevena recalls that crossing Lake Winnipeg his steamer put in to take on wood: "As it was an evil habit in those days to compose sonnets dedicated to Althea, Chloe, and other damsels of a youthful fancy, my object in wandering from the lakeside was to replenish my stocks of 'paper' by visiting the birch-trees which grew so abundantly in that region, and supplied me with thin sheets of bark-fibre admirably adapted for purposes of literature" (*Adventures*14). Hardy's and Trevena's writing materials represent a materialization of artistic creation that emphasizes their authors' connection to the surrounding natural world, almost as one encounters it in William Blake's "Introduction" to *Songs of Innocence* in which the poet "pluck'd a hollow reed / And I made a rural pen, / And I stain'd the water clear, / And I wrote my happy songs."

But nature, including human nature, is full of brutal experience and man is both complicitous in, and a victim of, harmful forces oblivious to his innocence or guilt. In Thomas Hardy's meditations on natural evils, his "purblind Doomsters" are the consequences of fickle fortune in a world ruled by a Will not merely indifferent, but unjust, morally blind, even cruelly mocking. In Trevena's *Furze the Cruel*, Abel Cain Weevil, the foster-father of Boodles, calls this power "the Brute." The Brute as the personification of cruelty, whether the intentional bullying of the destitute and weak by the villagers or the instinctive, amoral rabbit hunting of Aubrey's dog, is the existential givenness of facticity, source of all sadness. But one should not read Trevena's pessimism as indebtedness to Thomas Hardy nor, more radically, a bow to Arthur Schopenhauer's bleak philosophy that finds all human hopes fatally infected by a metaphysical hostility beyond nature, nor even to such concurrent movements as Naturalism or a dawning Nihilism that explain the indifference of the universe as a cosmic irony. Myrtle Henry, who corresponded with Trevena, said he considered Hardy "a pessimist; and apart from the fact that he had not read Hardy when the critics began calling him a Hardy disciple, he does not feel that the charge of pessimism can often be brought against him" (15).

One critic, summarizing Trevena's career, amusingly described his output as "written with much care and a most uncomfortable amount of knowledge of unpleasant things" ("Brief Notes" *7). The accent of Trevena's literary vision rests upon a profound sense that man can neither reach spiritual salvation by his own reason nor attain to happiness by his own agenda. Yet at the same time, because nature has so many facets and faces, he refuses to limit by denial the possibility of some unknown harmony resembling ordinances of the *Logos* within the flux of things and thoughts. In Trevena, the discords of a *diabolic* state of nature (Gk *dyo* two >*dia-* across, apart + *ballein* to throw) seem mystically balanced by a *symbolic* capacity to envision order (*syn/m-* together + *ballein*), the broken and "thrown apart" is made whole in and through a glimpse of the Transcendent that "throws together." Though in a poem, "To the Unknown God" (its original title is in Greek), even Hardy saw the Will growing "percipient with advance of days" and old wrongs "dying as of self-slaughter," yet more forcefully in Trevena than in Hardy the evolution of human consciousness may be pressing toward some paradise regained.

John Trevena began his writing career under his own name, Ernest Henham, with fiction such as *Tenebrae: A Novel* (1898) in the Gothic style of E. A. Poe's "The Fall of the House of Usher." But he reinvented both his style and career at the time of his anonymously published *A Pixy in Petticoats* (1906), a narrative of romance and legend neither grotesque nor decadent which proved popular in the United States as well as England. Trevena was very self-consciously *re*starting his career with this anonymous debut of *Pixy*. Thereafter, his novels were published under the pseudonym "John Trevena." Factual data on Henham/Trevena's career is scarce, but chapters two and three will flesh out a portrait of the man such as may enhance appreciation of his work, suggesting that the adoption of a pseudonym, which roughly coincided with his return from Canada to Devonshire's Dartmoor, was the major turning point in his career. At this time also his chronic respiratory ailment had worsened; elevated particulate levels caused reduced lung function and for Trevena triggered a chronic tubercular infection. He required the fresh air of higher elevations and avoidance of smoky industrial pollution, the "open-air treatment" mentioned in *Pixy* (41). Although the first of his consumptive protagonists, in *God, Man, and the Devil* (1897), went to Canada, all the others suffering from this disease go to Dartmoor. Even though it would be a mistake, certainly, to regard his Henham-era novels as lacking literary value, the later work, centered mainly in the Dartmoor area of Okehampton, is clearly of greatest significance. From first-hand experience Trevena portrays this area–part of the Duchy of Cornwall since 1240–as a uniquely diverse environment of rainy, wind-sweep moors and bogs, rivers, fields, neolithic ruins, farms with drunken farmers and villages with more drunks, and everywhere ineffectual vicars, enigmatic social customs, and dark superstitions. What especially adds to Trevena's forceful characterizations may have been his experiences in the colonial surroundings of Canada that stirred his sympathy for the native North Americans, making him particularly aware of the abject and destitute conditions of the local inhabitants on Dartmoor. It has been noted that social development within the colonies outstripped the British homeland by erasing the locked-down class system–one instantly sees the truth of this in the empire romances of Haggard, Mitford, or Glanville. Yet Trevena despised the weaknesses of the Dartmoor inhabitants; and like the rocks which give *Granite*(1909) its title, the author is devoid of any sentimental pity and can be as ruthless as fate itself. His tone is grimly grey; his humor, often bitter.

One suspects Trevena's health-enforced intention was to outstrip the popular regional novelist of the West Country, Eden Phillpotts, whose well-received *Children of the Mist* (1898) and other novels were in those days in high favor. Both Trevena and Phillpotts chronicle provincial lifeways more pagan than Christian, where inessentials give way in the face of nature to the intense elemental issues of birth, love, hate, death. In connection with the moorland setting, both also had, as was noted, "the slow, unhurried method, the digression to linger with Nature, the quaint and queer types of humanity that throng their pages" (Colbron 327; "Novels" 652). But if each waxed poetic at times, Trevena accented the harrowing and elegiac whereas Phillpotts tended toward the benign and cheerful. Professor Frederic Taber Cooper's comparison in 1912 is finally the most effective:

> in each that same artistic sense of . . . the wonderful softness of nature, seen through a shimmering haze of English sunshine, or a slanting veil of English rain. But when it comes to the human life in the stories, one feels at once how radically far apart these two authors really are. Both of them picture a phase of the English peasantry; . . . the portraiture of each is a fine example of honest and unsparing realism. And yet the difference between these two authors is fundamental, because it is the difference of their point of view. Mr. Phillpotts identifies himself with the people of whom he writes. He and his characters and his readers are all held together in one big, universal bond of understanding and pity. . . . John Trevena, on the contrary, remains always an alien. The natives are always to him objects of special study, but rather in the spirit with which a botanist studies a new species of lichen than with any sense of the brotherhood of man. . . . It is not too much to say that one actually suffers more over the unconscious cruelty of nature and the inhumanity of man in Mr. Trevena's pages than in any of the more sympathetic pictures of life that Mr. Phillpotts has given us. . . . Mr. Trevena's attitude is quite indifferently objective; he is not the compassionate Samaritan, but the vivisectionist, finding an absorbing interest even in suffering and disease and death. (326-328).

A reviewer of Phillpotts wrote, "He does not have the strength and fierceness of John Trevena . . . but he does have larger elements of popularity. Trevena will never be widely read; there is something forbidding in his books. One is glad to have read them; Trevena will have a small audience, always eager to sample the hard-rock-like magic of such books as 'Granite' and 'Furze,' but the audience will be limited. Mr. Phillpotts should possess a larger group of readers, for his narrative vein is more facile" ("Phillpotts" 7, 10). Agreeing that their fiction grows out of a specific topographical setting, Paul Jordan-Smith, the literary editor of the *Los Angles Times*, maintained that "anything Eden Phillpotts could do well, Trevena can do better. His descriptions of Dartmoor are more varied and colorful; his characterizations more vivid and less typified; his humor more spontaneous" (*For the Love of Books* 82). It has been remarked that Hardy's novels are visually cinematic;

Trevena's by contrast are like dark Blakean engravings–their chiaroscuro intensified by a brutal Goyaesque realism that nests on the depths of the subconscious: scenes such as Will Yeo finding his friend's body eaten by rats or the foul odor emanating from the well of Mrs. Fuzzey, the midwife, down which she threw the babies of unwed mothers. Although Trevena may not have read Arnold Bennett or the French novels of Gustave Flaubert, Honoré de Balzac or stories of Guy de Maupassant, he clearly was working along the same lines without abandoning the Romantic and mystical premises of his art.

Trevena employs innovative fictional techniques–for that era perhaps even avant-garde–such as juxtaposing a robust realism with dark comedy and pathos, or imbricating local legends and folklore with his main plot-action. In fictional realism, sight is the dominant sense in describing the world; but in Trevena the visual environment and its actions are filtered by the intricacies of temperament and consciousness, the turns and twists of interiority. If most fictional worlds are understood through tightly linked moments of description and drama, there are times also when the reader must be separated from that imagined reality to be shown something new in a more comprehensive way by resources outside "traditional" forms of storytelling; that is, by expository correlations and commentary interpreting ideas or threads of emerging concepts. Trevena's plot-action is almost a background to the circumstantial scenes that are minutely executed in the foreground: his story can become tenuous, lightly spread out; his characters are the mosaic tesserae producing patterns "moving with quiet force and undramatic bearing." Walter Pater, probably under the influence of Montaigne and Sainte-Beuve, once described his fiction as presenting not an action or a story but a character, personality revealed in outward detail. Trevena'semphasis is also less on immediate gesture, utterance, or dramatic events than on finely discriminated details of setting, feelings, sensations, and intuitions. Exterior and interior worlds engage in a duet between the visual and its psychological equivalents. This modernist emphasis upon the protagonist's inner experiences as a spectator of events rather than the hero of an action challenges the idea that humans exist only by what they do, and extends or transforms that literalism to provide–if not a "self" as defined by full-blown epiphanic moments of awareness–at least a new, deeper way of understanding selfhood in terms of what it beholds.

Readers could appreciate Trevena's vivid character descriptions, his poetically atmospheric delineations or personifications of the forces of nature, and his powerful and at times weirdly nightmarish atmosphere and visionary symbolism. But readers also expected the author to be strict in sticking to the main narrative (as today writers of film scripts still must do). The interpretive frameworks and analytic vocabulary of popular readers were inadequate to understand Trevena's attempts to capture the "quiddity" of Dartmoor experience by, for example, techniques of juxtaposition focused on numerous overlapping, interwoven images and happenings which are anything but unconnected events or careless digressions. Here is how such critical responsestypically unfolded in reviews:

> These books are strikingly reminiscent of Thomas Hardy's works, Nature in them being treated never of secondary importance, and always of a sinister dynamic power. The structure of the books is not that of a single unit; instead they are a vivid patchwork of color, brilliant portraiture, flashes of drama, amazing if sometimes purposeless observation, and not infrequently the commonplaces of the mediocre novel. The latest novel of Trevena's to be discussed is "Wintering Hay" (Kennerley). In reviewing it, E. F. Edgett in the *Boston Transcript* points out some of the weaknesses of Trevena's work:
>
> "He writes with the freedom of one who is independent of all the rules and regulations of fiction. He seems indeed deliberately to rebel against them, and to be striving to make his stories chaotic and formless. It is difficult, even impossible, at times to follow him intelligently, and more than once during the course of his long novels the reader wonders whether Mr. Trevena is not losing himself in a maze of human complications and wandering hither and thither in a vain effort to extricate himself. Is his peculiar manner simply a conscious and persistent effort to reproduce the chaos of life, or is it due to his inability skilfully to avail himself of the resources of that constructive technique which every novelist should have at his command? These are the questions that we are continually asking during a reading of Mr. Trevena's novels.
>
> "From 'Furze the Cruel' to 'Wintering Hay,' as Mr. Trevena's novels have come to us from England, we have been in a con-

stant state of bewilderment. At successive moments during our reading of him he appears to be a genius and a charlatan, an artist and an incompetent, a man of great knowledge and a man of little wisdom. But never at any time is there doubt of his originality or a suspicion that his work is not the expression of a unique individuality. He himself is a mystery."

> Trevena, we must conclude, surpasses at individual portraiture, giving words free rein when he describes one of his carefully studied characters of Dartmoor. "His isolated episodes glow with a colorful significance," writes Mr. Edgett. If at times he fails to convince, his sin is one of omission rather than of emphasis. ("Novelist" 429)

In the eighth of his *Discourses* (1769-90), Sir Joshua Reynolds remarks of novelty, variety, and contrast that "those qualities, . . . if they are carried to excess, become defects" (1:440). The problem becomes what constitutes "excess" decade by decade, school by school, critic by critic in any given work alleged to have the defects of its qualities. The classic example of technique outrunning theory in Trevena's lifetime was the work of G.M. Hopkins, the introverted poet who linked his natural environment to a spiritual order and, like Trevena, wrote in the line of Romanticism to Symbolism and beyond to Modernism. Hopkins saw only a few poems published in his lifetime until finally in1918 the time was ripe to reclaim him from years of obscurity.

In connection with Trevena another specific failure of critical insight was that readers somewhat too hastily concluded his characters lacked the complexity of internal psychological conflict and development. As analysis of John Burrough in *Pixy*, Cyril Rossingall in *Wintering Hay,* John Anger in *Sleeping Waters* and others makes clear, this is so wrong one has to admit, as E. F. Edgett claimed, Trevena's readers did not "follow him intelligently." For example, the most fascinating instances of internal conflicts may be characters who cannot accommodate to the binary difference by which people are split exclusively into only two sexes and genders. Among Trevena's characters are numerous figures of bisexuality and unconventional gender roles, including Thirza Billacott in *Sleeping Waters;* both Mary Tavy, the giantess, and Aubrey Bellamie, with a face like a girl, in *Furze*; Sal Lampey who manhandles Coneybear in *Arminel*; the transvestite disguise of

Peter-Cherry, "son and daughter in one body" in *Moyle Church-Town* (58); the figure in *Wintering Hay* of James Joll called Jane, who is legally female but actually male (55), which created issues with his tombstone (435); and in *Pixy* both Poltesco, Beatrice's "nurse" who is a fisherman (159), and Beatrice herself who insists that she become Burrough's "pal Bill" (237). Beatrice's re-gendered self, almost as homoerotic as that of Boodles who envisions sleeping with a female as a stand-in for her lost Aubrey, may be an attempt to keep Burrough's desire at bay. Or does Beatrice want to be a man so she can have a homoerotic relationship with another male? At least it removes the conventional role of spouses from the emotional equation. In *Heather*, one of Trevena's most explicit passages on sexual identity points both to his character's bisexuality and to his own authorial progressiveness mixed with a religious or, more likely, a biological reservation. Here again the girl is called Billy by her female companion:

> "I don't want you to marry, little Bill. I want to have you myself."
>
> Winnie wondered at that. She knew nothing of the love which goes out to its own sex and almost disregards the other; an unnatural and barren kind of love, and yet as enduring as any. (218)

Trevena defines the speaker as "a handsome brown girl, not by any means sexless, but on the contrary strongly bi-sexual. She had been bisected as it were, divided into two equal parts, one feminine, the other masculine" (262).

Moreover, criticism that posits a failure of internal conflict also overlooks another sort of conflict that is not psychologically internal but principally structural, the conflict between policies and institutions that creates obstacles to economic and social equality. Trevena questions conceptual oppositions that legitimize divergent social classes. These age old social-structural conflicts culminated for him in Britain's "Age of Empire," a phrase that conjures up the optimism and progress that began in the technological triumphs after the Industrial Revolution, continued with the nineteenth-century scientific discoveries, and that culminated in an empire on which "the sun never sets." But the age also was associated with unsettling cultural transformations, not just repression and narrow moralism or poverty and crime, but a class system that during the Edwardian era still remained rigid even though economic and social changes were bringing greater mobility than in the preceding Victorian period. In consequence of rapid industrialization and increasing economic opportunities for women and the poor, together with the rise of socialism and trade unionism, progress for the working class and the status of women steadily moved to the forefront of discussion. Trevena, however, saw a downside to contemporary leadership that failed to address the flaws in democracy. He saw politicians, lacking moderation and tempted by power for its own sake, leading England into decline. By contrast, John Ruskin's *Lectures on Art* (1873) served as a *locus classicus* for an unquestioning patriotism by which Britain would enrich the rest of the world out of her culture and traditions–and be enriched by the ransacking of foreign resources. In H. G. Wells's *War of the Worlds* (1898) both ethnocentric British imperialists and scientific researchers observing protozoans are no different from the Martians studying earth. Wells implies that the technologically superior Martian invaders are only the British imperialists themselves in another guise–each overconfident and ready for a fall.

Trevena's political fantasy of England conquered and ruled by Japan, *The Reign of the Saints* (1911), will be understood by the intelligent reader as just this sort of a reverse parable of English imperialism, crystallizing current fears about the discipline and physical vigor of the populace:

> You know, better than the writer, what befalls the country which demands all the luxury that civilization can offer, which squanders money heedlessly, develops an abnormal passion for amusements, rebels against sound government, shirks military service, shrugs its shoulders at the falling birth-rate, professes no religion except in name and outward show, and feasts while the Goths are waiting at the gates. (Preface vi)

With a sort of Carlylean humor, Trevena dedicates *Reign of the Saints* to those "deaf" to political campaigns, "dumb" to the polling-booths, and "blind" to the newspapers which espouse socialism and false democracy. He believed that false democracy is created by the arrogant assumptions of the ruling classes who think that right of birth entitles them to exercise all the powers of the citizenry. A democratic façade is not as vulgar as tyranny, but it too victimizes by means of enforced class values–the customs, institutions, and laws of the land.

Perhaps Henham/Trevena considered such illusory equality of rights and privileges more difficult to combat than some form of foreign conquest; at any rate, according to Exeter archives he was not registered on the electorate lists, so he apparently never voted during his stay on Dartmoor–"dumb" to the polling-booth. Trevena, not convinced of the value of government by the people, offers no explicit ideological solution other than appearing sympathetic to monarchy. In *Reign of the Saints* a king whose power comes from nature and divinity is proclaimed in Dartmoor, from which historically dukes had become kings. But history may have given Trevena another model of successful polity–benevolent governance as articulated by Plato in *The Republic*. Having witnessed uncontrolled democracy's execution of Socrates his master, Plato appears disenchanted with the democratic ideal and proposes that only a philosopher-King can rule society, for only such a figure can work toward society's common good while avoiding influences from baser sources. A more recent expression of "social feudalism" had been Thomas Carlyle's criticism of democracy and its inability to identify fit leaders to govern which entailed suffering their absence. At any rate, Trevena's radical social satire and his conservative attack on socialism's promotion of material selfishness are easily reconciled in the symbolic vision(if not taken too literally) of a philosopher-king functioning as a wise father who seeks not his own interests but the common welfare of all inhabitants, including the marginalized poor, battered women, unwanted infants, the unoffending feeble-minded, and the abused population of the animal kingdom.

How can such a writer as Trevena, a bold critic of social inequity and exponent of what the poet G. M. Hopkins saw as a divine pattern and energy in nature, be so neglected today? In the middle of the nineteenth century, Edward Bulwer-Lytton in his "Dedicatory Epistle" to *The Last of the Barons* (1843) defined fiction of the "Intellectual School" as a genre requiring a longer attention span and a higher level of understanding owing to the development of character and plot through subtlety of form and content rather than primarily through direct action–an observation later fashionably reworked in Roland Barthes's *S/Z* (1970). Though rather windy by current standards, Bulwer's contrast of the "Familiar" (or mimetic) and "Intellectual" styles (requiring serious thought) explains why some of us still require undergraduates to read what they would prefer to avoid:

> To my mind, a writer['s] . . . first care should be the conception of a whole as lofty as his intellect can grasp, as harmonious and complete as his art can accomplish; his second care, the character of the interest which the details are intended to sustain. The Intellectual will probably never be the most widely popular for . . . its greatest excellences . . . are not the most obvious to the many. . . .The literary history of the day consists of a series of judgments set aside. But this uncertainty must more essentially betide every student [L. *studere* push on, be zealous, to apply oneself], however lowly, in the school I have called the Intellectual, which must ever be more or less at variance with the popular canons. It is its hard necessity to vex and disturb the lazy quietude of vulgar taste; for unless it did so, it could neither elevate nor move, . . . seeking in action the movement of the grander passions or the subtler springs of conduct, seeking in repose the colouring of intellectual beauty. The absence or presence of the Ideal! But every one can judge of the merit of the first, for it is of the Familiar school; it requires a connoisseur to see the merit of the last, for it is of the Intellectual. (xii)

From Bulwer's point of view, Trevena's manifest regionalism thus becomes a vehicle for underlying multiple layers of intellectual engagement, but certainly no assurance of an ongoing *popular* success.

The critical reception of Trevena's novels was enthusiastic, emphatic in praise, though at times expressing a genteel intimidation by the harshness of Trevena's scenes and repugnant characters. When *Furze the Cruel* appeared in 1907, the *Academy* found Trevena "as cruel as his own Furze; he is relentless in the grim matter-of-fact horror of his art." The reviewer declared it darker than Kingsley's *Yeast* and as honest as Zola's *La Terre*: "It is always difficult to define what constitutes greatness in any form of art; but when greatness exists it is easy to discover. 'Furze the Cruel' is undoubtedly a great book–almost a masterpiece"(68). The

Dundee Advertiser prognosticated that "'Furze the Cruel' will rank in the forefront of modern fiction"("Some Press Opinions" [ii]). The *Athenæum* said it was a book not easily read and not easily forgotten: "The characters live and move, and are so nicely balanced in their relations as to make them seem the result of their environment" ("Fiction" 684). A review in *The New York Times* (1908) hailed his heroines as triumphs of characterization; and a subsequent review in the same paper found Trevena "unquestionably one of the most notable of living writers" ("New Year Fiction" 55), a sentiment the paper iterated yet again nearly two years later. The *Boston Transcript* reviewer E. F. Edgett had noted that because of Trevena's intricate profusion of characters and incidents "he looms large in the English fiction of the present moment, and that he bids fair to hold a high place in its future. No one can read him without being impressed by the force of his imagination, and no matter how much he may annoy and amaze us at times by his eccentricity, we cannot fail to see in him the genius that perhaps is all the greater because it is unregulated. He is a novelist to be read, to be studied and to be discussed" (8). And the prestigious *Current Opinion*–that was more than willing to point out faults–opened a review with this assessment:

> Out of every hundred novels published during the year, we read in the book review of the New York Times, at least seventy-five are advertized as "big." "Out of the seventy-five there are occasionally two or three which actually deserve to be thus classified, and among these few rank the works of that very unusual writer, John Trevena." Other reviewers have been likewise impressed by the novels of Trevena, which are being published in the United States in rapid succession by Mitchell Kennerley. The Boston Herald sets him beside Galsworthy, De Morgan, Bennett and Wells, and thinks that "the uniform quality of his work will place him above any of these." Other critics are equally enthusiastic. (429)

In summing up the case for Trevena's accomplishment, one could do worse than cite a mere three sentences from the *Los Angeles Times*: "Russia has produced the most powerful novelists. Beside Turgenief and Dostoievsky we know of no American and but one Englishman who is fairly entitled to a place. John Trevena alone writes with the force, the dynamic power of the brooding, Slavic titans" ("A Powerful Novel" AB4). Like Dostoyevsky in an earlier generation, Trevena uses imaginative literature to explore philosophical and psychological dimensions; and his ideational content is not deployed merely to clarify a specific event nor limited to the exposition of essential background. And, like his Russian predecessors, his conceptual components do not cloud artistic subtlety or clarity by inartistically overwhelming or obscuring the visual elements. With reviews like those above, Trevena should have felt as if he were acquiring a knighthood or a halo of intellectual sainthood that would hover around him throughout his life and forever beyond. Yet as the following chapters make clear, by the end of his life Trevena seems, much like Hopkins, to have despaired of an audience, then or afterwards.

A possible reason for his subsequent comparative obscurity emerges if one connects the reviewer's likening of Trevena to the "Slavic titans" with Virginia Woolf's reference concerning Russian narratives. In "Modern Fiction" (1919; revised 1925), Woolf observed that the best modern English fiction was influenced by the spirituality of Russian literature–a fiction that like hers and that of Joyce explored the inner world of the mind's perceptions as well as the world of the heart. Only a year or two after the *Los Angeles Times* review of Trevena, Woolf and James Joyce published their first novels. Could it be that this avant-garde wave swept Trevena from the stage, a bona fide predecessor but too much the outsider to be remembered as an innovator? Later in this study, I will compare some of Trevena's fiction to that of Walter Pater, the founder of British aestheticism and a critical influence on the new psychological novel. Sensing the uniqueness of individual experience as basic to fiction, Pater's imaginary portraits were forerunners of the "new form" for the novel that Woolf, Joyce, Joseph Conrad and others desired to find. They expressed their indebtedness to Pater, of course, who discreetly networked from Oxford, Britain's intellectual center; Trevena however lived in near isolation on the moors of Devon; and although he had "travelled about the world" (*Adventures* 59), he shunned publicity.

CHAPTER 2

E.G. HENHAM | *TENEBRAE* (1898)

Born on 14 December 1870 in the London suburb of Lower Norwood, John Trevena's actual name was Thomas Ernest George Henham. He was the fourth child, the only son of Thomas (1834–1871) and Emily Henham, *née* Stapleton (1833–1876). Aside from a few facts here and there, no real biographical profile of the author's life had appeared until three years ago (Monsman vi-xii, xviii-xx); it was almost as if he had no life outside of his own head. The time-tested way of beginning biographical research is with obituaries, but Trevena was so forgotten that even his date ofdeath, 1948, was long in error. Owning to Lucien Leclaire's *A General Analytical Bibliography of the Regional Novelists in the British*(1954), Trevena's death had been entered in bibliographic files (when given at all) as 1946. At the time of his birth, the family had been living in the Greater London borough of Lambeth St. Mary. According to his *Who's Who* entries (1928–1944), he designates his birth as posthumous. Duane Searle states on the basis of genealogical research that his father died on 1 May 1871 while Henham was yet only a few months old (Trevena, "Short Stories" 1); his mother remarried but died when the boy was a five-year-old. By the age of ten he was at "The Vicarage" with his uncle William Henham, the Vicar of Streatley since 1880, and his aunt Millicent. E.W. Martin, a local historian who corresponded and spoke directly with the elderly Trevena, writes:

> His youth was a period of unhappiness. His parents died when he was very young and the boy found himself left in the care of relatives.[1] "I very nearly became another Oliver Twist. Much better for me had I been left in some orphanage, but, unhappily, I was adopted by an uncle (a country clergyman–a man of God)." Trevena will not dwell upon those years; yet it is certain that here was the soil in which his talent ripened;

1. The Reverend William Townsend Henham was born about 1828; graduated from Christ's College, Cambridge in 1851; ordained that same year and held various curacies from 1851 until 1880 when he became Vicar of St. Mary's Church, Streatley, Berkshire, Diocese of Oxford. He married Millicent Caroline Powys 4 October 1870 at Alderbury, Wiltshire, and he died in 1900.

without normal human contacts, deprived of affection, Trevena's imagination began to work and he weaved stories thatpictured a happier future. (87)

One suspects covert autobiographical touches are everywhere in Trevena's writing, as when George Brunacombe in *Heather* confides to the Rector: "when I was a child . . . I was frightened to death by accounts of hell. I dared not pass the blacksmith's shop because I thought that was hell" (342).

In the opening pages of his memoir-like*Adventures Among Wild Flowers*, Trevena credited "the old gentleman," his uncle, with giving him "a practical interest in the life of plants" (2). Possibly only an ironist like Trevena could combine in a title "adventures" and "flowers"–with the blossoms modified by "wild"! Trevena's personal recollections of his love for delicate wild flowers is here brilliantly invoked by means of a nostalgic memory of their blue color:

> A white hill and a blue flower. An old gentleman standing before the shrubberies of the vicarage, looking down upon a little person of twelve years old, and saying, "So you think you can find the blue flower. I will give you a shilling for every blossom you bring back."
>
> The romance of a plant-collector began that day when I went up into the mountain to look for the flower of good fortune; not the speedwell of myth, but the living and breathing Easter wind flower, the Pasque anemone,[2] called by botanists *pulsatilla*; and the mountain was only one of the chalk uplands of the Berkshire downs, covered more thickly then than now with upright junipers like dusky sentinels, and pitted with dew-ponds full of newts. A wonderful place for twelve-year-old eyes, and a brain saturated with Grimm and Andersen.
>
> Is it necessary to insist upon the success of that expedition? Neither flower nor fairy can hide from the eyes of childhood. I walked in a straight line to the garden of Pasque Flowers, gathered as many as I could carry in comfort, and returned dreaming to the old gentleman, who knew a good deal of

2. The common Speedwell (*Veronica filiformis*) received its name from St. Veronica who wiped Christ's face on his way to Calvary; and because Passover and Easter coincide, the "windflower" which blooms around that time of year is called the Pasque (a form of *pascha*, passover) or Easter flower.

botany, and regarded *Anemone pulsatilla* as a rarity which he might search for all day and never find. But then, he was not twelve years old.

Entering the study I released a purple cascade upon his sermon paper; while he drew on his spectacles and fingered the hairy petals; until convinced the flowers were genuine he went through the heap and, having come to the decision that sixty blooms were good specimens, he handed me three sovereigns, which immense sum of money would probably have been squandered upon doughnuts and nougat, had not authority intervened and diverted the capital into educational channels, as represented by a magic lantern and set of fretwork tools.

That money did me a great deal of good, because it was earned worthily. It gave me a practical interest in the life of plants, and showed me that the stories I was so fond of reading were not all fairy-tales. The blue flower did indeed bring happiness.[3] In the tales a lonely traveller would gather the flower, and immediately the rocks opened, and he was invited to enter the mountain and fill his pockets with gold. In my own experience the discovery of the blue flower brought a fortune; at least it was a fortune to a child. Even during the earliest years money appears to bring a great deal of happiness. Those three sovereigns were spent upon things which had no influence whatever, and possessed only a passing interest; but the means by which they had been earned made a permanent impression. The main interest of a man's life was created by the chance ramble of a child.

We are often ashamed of our humanity, and truly the kind of sentiment which makes us cling to a scrap of ribbon or a faded flower may become a hindrance in the battle for existence. I still preserve one of those sixty anemones pressed in an old Bible as thin and dry as wafer: seen in twilight sometimes the beautiful blue spirit appears to haunt the petals. It is difficult to destroy such trifles, even when no personal sentiment is attached to them. (1-3)

One of Henham's earliest projects was to have been a book about his garden of "stolen" plants–wild ones, snatched wherever.

---

3. Novalis (Georg von Hardenberg) named the Romantic longing for happiness *die blaue Blume*,"the blue flower."

He attended St. Edward's School, Oxford–a "little white-faced boy in his ugly braided suit, fashionable in stiff Victorian days" (186)–and at fifteen while at school began to submit work to publishers. "Between the ages of twelve and seventeen," he writes, "I have a clear recollection of commencing two novels, one five-act tragedy, an epic poem, a treatise upon engineering (with illustrations and diagrams by the author), and a pamphlet upon Sanitary Methods as applied to Public Schools, not to mention at length various short stories dealing with murders and revenants of the moated grange" (17). Once, a few miles above Oxford at Godstow, at some excavations in the graveyard of a twelfth-century nunnery where Fair Rosamond had been kept by her royal lover, Henry II, Trevena and a schoolmate raked out "various mediæval fragments," then wound up their day "by a game of catch with the skull of some poor old nun. . . . Elderly people wrote to the press complaining of the 'scenes of blasphemy,' and one mentioned he had seen with his own eyes 'two little monsters playing at catch with a human skull,' a memory which I still shudder at" (64). According to Searle he attended St Edward's "between 1881 and Easter 1890. . . . During 1886, when he was 16 years old, Henham became seriously ill with an unspecified disease" (2).[4] This likely marked the inception of his life-long tuberculosis.

In the recollection of his first love for the fairer sex, Trevena's account of his affection for blue wild flowers is continued by the use of blue for ribbons and eyes:

> Sentiment known as first love drew me back to the chalk hills at the age of sixteen, but I was not in the mood to look for blue flowers. Indeed memory assures me it was summer, the time of hairbells, when the anemones would have been nestling down asleep. I was far more anxious to lead my fair companion to the dew-ponds, that I might impress her by my skill in catching newts; and, being very much in love, I probably tried to slip one of the cold reptiles into her shrinking hand. Memory presents few clear outlines of that day, because there was nothing lasting about the sentiment; for first love is a

4. Searle's preface to his edition of Henham/Trevena's short stories provides dates and an interesting account of the author's encounter with a ghost; however, the editor fails to cite Trevena's own short story collection, *Written in the Rain* (1910), thereby overlooking several important stories and misdating others.

> plant without roots, even though the bloom has a marvellous fragrance; but I do remember that we grew suddenly shy, and she walked upon one side of the junipers while I walked upon the other. And upon returning we were ushered into the presence of the old gentleman who had paid a good price for the anemones to receive sentence and punishment, for discipline was strict in those days, and the schoolgirl who wilfully ran away from her chaperon was regarded as second in wickedness only to the boy who had tempted her to stray.
>
> 'You will never be worthy to follow me as vicar of this parish,' said the old gentleman, as his eyes wandered towards that terrible black ruler. And he was right. How fortunate it is our wishes are not granted! Still it was fine to be in love. One could do well at the sports, or knock up fifty at cricket, when she was looking on; but to go out collecting wild flowers seemed at that period an occupation for the maiden aunts. Valentines were the rule in those days, but you might only guess at the identity of the sender, because it was not lawful to recognise the handwriting upon the envelope nor to decipher the postmark. So I can only surmise that a certain little laced picture of two doves tied together with blue ribbons was sent by my companion of Wildflower Hill; although I am free to confess I sent her a most barbaric representation of two hearts skewered upon an arrow. A good many years afterwards we met, but found each other uninteresting. She was accompanied by a dear little daughter with blue eyes for memories. (3-5)

A sad old man had told the young boy, "The blue periwinkle is for memories"; but the white is for "happy memories" (186). Trevena recalls that as a schoolboy it was "near Godstow and leafy Wytham I began to study nature, chiefly I fear in the form of consigning newts to glass bottles, and eating minnows raw–for that was a hungry period–and it was certainly there I received a kind of barbaric interest in the flowers" (63). This "hungry period" coincided roughly both with dew-pond newt collecting alongside his "fair companion" and with his attack of respiratory disease or tubercular infection; each occurred in his sixteenth year.

E.W. Martin summarizes Trevena's comments on Canada:

> After his school days he was sent to a farm in North-West Canada, where life in the open air and in a new country was most attractive to him. Without money, he was soon in difficulties, and finally entered a law office, managing to exist on

> fifteen dollars a month until the lawyers to which he was articled discovered that he wrote poetry in his spare time, and for this grave offence they quite illegally cancelled his articles and cast him adrift. He came back to London and resided in Camden Town. When the rush to the Yukonstarted [1897] Trevena found that his fortunes were mending, for he was able to write about life in Canada, and there was a market for his books. (87-88)

The fact is confirmed in Trevena's own words in *Who's Who* that his early adulthood was spent in Canada, including the University of Manitoba (though he does not appear in Alumni records), with stints as "cowboy and student, lumberman and poet; articled to lawyer who cancelled articles upon discovering that he was in the habit of contributing poems to the local press; consumption throughout life, disease became active in 1903, and since then he has been compelled to live more or less in seclusion." His dismissal by the lawyer, judging from his subsequent fiction, seems to have given him a lifelong dislike of the legal profession, much like Shakespeare's.Searle cites *Henderson's Manitoba Directory* (1894) as listing Henham attending St. John's College (3), one of the founding colleges in the University of Manitoba, with strong connections to the Anglican Church.

The "Henham" novels, eight in all, primarily share a Canadian background and were published between 1897 and 1907. Of the genesis of his novel, *Menoah* (1897), a story of the Canadian North-West Rebellion, Henham writes that it "dwells upon what was undoubtedly one of the principal reasons for the revolt, viz., the unscrupulous treatment of the Indian women by the white invaders":

> The writer was present in the riverside town of St Boniface [Winnipeg]on a certain still evening during the August of 1894. There all the houses, and even the trees that lined the streets, were heavily draped in black; men and women passed slowly with heads uncovered and attitude of grief; it was as though each had lost his or her nearest and dearest relative. . . . For the Archbishop lay dead in the Cathedral. Later, when the sun was setting over this place of universal grief, the writer came within the dark building, crept up a winding stairway, to find himself confronted suddenly by a singularly solemn spectacle. Before the altar, robed in full pontificals, sat in State the

> dead Archbishop, while lamps flickered solemnly, and muttered intercessions arose from the trembling lips of a ring of kneeling priests. . . . The writer came at length to the side of the dead prelate, and bent to reverently kiss the cold gloved hand of the mighty dead. Then he departed, with a silent resolve to do such justice as he could to the memory of this beloved Father and Pastor, who had worked so nobly for the welfare of the country of his adoption. (Prefatory Note)

These novels are variously propagandistic (against divorce, against unjust dealings with the Indians) or romantic and heroic tales (one of an Indian maiden's love and two others of feuds between Indians and settlers) or spiritualistic narratives (a psychological horror story, a haunted house with mystic influences, and a tale of reincarnation).

During this decade Henham also published short stories in some of the best British literary periodicals: *Macmillan's*, *The Cornhill Magazine*, *The Illustrated London News*, *The Living Age*, *Cassell's Magazine*, and *Temple Bar*, among others. His description of the northwest prairies of Canada is vivid: "Away on all sides extended the snow-covered wastes, broken here and there by dark-green fir bluffs, their tresses blue with ice. Not a man, not an animal, nor bird, nor insect could be seen for miles. But what of that? It is glorious to see the pale blue sky spotted with fragile cirri, to watch the frost dancing around, and to feel the sharp prick of the crystals against the exposed cheeks and nose, and to hear the comfortable swish of the sleigh as it slid along, and the quick breathing of the dogs" (*Written . . . Rain* 184). He originally published this as "The Frozen Man" in the *Cornhill Magazine* (October 1897); his 1910 revision of it incorporated one entirely new scene and one gruesome event from another Henham tale of the prairie, "A Newspaper Stopgap" in the *Cornhill Magazine* (January1900). These Canadian stories may be among his best, essentially tales from colonial life, many with an overtone of strange accidents or adventures. "Talbot" of the Hudson Bay Company is the author's persona in a number of these narratives woven around travels in the region of Fort Qu'Appelleat a hub of trading trailswhere the Hudson Bay district headquarters, and the governmental Indian Department agent were located. The name and employment of this first person narrator was deleted in his

1910 story collection. Details from Henham's own experiences or his recollections of incidents recounted in newspapers and saloons doubtless are used to flesh out Talbot's narratives on the rigors of winter on the prairie or even for the law office in *Sleeping Waters*. Also very fine are several stories situated in Dartmoor, particularly "Old Bailey's Wooing" (1903), "The Sound of Ladybrook Water" (1913), and "By Violence" (before 1910). The theme of the gentleman often fallen on hard times because of alcoholism recurs in several pen-portraits of wasted human talent. When hauntings or ghosts become the theme, almost invariably the supernatural effects are found to have a satisfying natural/scientific explanation. The one exception is his oddest and finest fantastic story of ants taking vengeance on an evil man, "Bugs and Other Things" (before 1910), that is possibly set either in northwestern Ontario along a fifty mile river-chain of lakes or around Lake Winnipeg. The wry humor with which he describes the first mouthful of river water by a thirsty young lady as tasting "of various orders of reptiles" (*Written . . . Rain* 48) is typical of the author's backwoods seasoning. Trevena's finest work of semi-fiction is "Matrimony" (1910), which he characterizes as "not a story, but an attempt to reproduce the marriage service of the mediæval church,"written, one supposes, with his own approaching nuptials in mind (v).

As an example of his "pre-Trevena" mind-set, Henham's early psychological horror story, *Tenebrae: A Novel* (1898), deserves some attention. Its basic Gothic premise derives from Old Norse skaldic and Eddaic poetry; namely, that the self is both a human body (*lich*) and an enveloping spirit (*hug*) from which a second body belonging to each individual is formed, a *doppelgänger* ("astral" body is the theosophical term) that sooner or later may become strong enough to take the visible form of an animal or other personal emblem (not excluding the arthropods of this novel). This *hug* is separate from its physical twin but follows like a shadow–and when seen is often a portent of approaching death. Henham wrote *Tenebrae* toward the end of an exceptionally fertile resurgence of Gothic fiction: *Dr. Jekyll and Mr. Hyde* (1886), *The Picture of Dorian Gray* (1890-91), *The Island of Dr. Moreau* (1896), and *Dracula* (1897). Oddly, Henham's publisher, Skeffington and Son, specialized in theology, children's picture books, and (perhaps not the father's side of the business) novels of lurid sins and melodramatic suicides. The novel was issued in crown octavo with a cover that evoked the novel's "darkness" theme, its title with stars, clouds, prominent sailing owl and flying bat are all done in black and orange on a sage-green cloth binding. Were it not for its psychological ambiguities, *Tenebrae* might be thought to be either *homage* to E.A. Poe's works aimed at mass-market tastes–indeed, one does suspect it grew into a full blown novel from a lengthy story in situation and imagery much like "The Fall of the House of Usher" (1839-40)–or, for the sake of satirical humor, a deliberate *parody* of Poe's Gothic effects and insane narrators. In either such case one might then adapt the wry opening sentence of Arthur Symons's review of Francis Thompson's first volume: "If Crashaw, Shelley, Donne, Marvell, Mr. Patmore and some other poets had not existed, Mr. Francis Thompson would be a poet of remarkable novelty" (Rev. of *Poems* 143). But the likeliest possibility is neither homage nor parody; rather, we have covert self-expression touching personal and cultural anxieties so unmentionable that the cloak of Gothic fiction was the safest means by which they might be explored. In Victorian society (and, one might add, almost any other culture) those who can express what, and when, and where was a closely controlled matter of precept and proscription. It has been observed, for example, that after the French Revolution an expressed wish for the death of any authority-figure, particularly the father, was socially taboo because it renewed anxieties about disruption and chaos. Our contemporary society is so much more open that often only legalities prompt distancing techniques, such as euphemisms in polite society or the not infrequently hypocritical asseveration that "any resemblance to actual events or persons, living or dead, is entirely coincidental."

One reader called this novel "a sort of morbid dream" (Tanguy12). Henham's dark Romanticism explores the violence and aberrant sexuality of the narrator, an individual perversely self-destructive, a social outcast racked with personal fears, and one for whom the supernatural is hellishly hallucinatory. His dawning realization–to give a nod to Giovanni Palestrina's *Peccantem Me*–is the somewhat less-than-cheerful realization that "there is no redemption in hell." In the handling of these somber Gothic themes, Henham is by turns serious and comic, very much in the tradition of Walpole's *Castle of Otranto* (1764) or *The Mysterious*

Mother (1791) with their exaggerated intensity of warped desire turned violent. But his story, apart from Poe's influence, recalls especially the unapologetic supernatural staginess of M.G. Lewis's *The Monk* (1796), described by Francis Jeffrey as a "mixture of extravagance and jocularity which has impressed most of his writings with the character of a sort of farcical horror" (Rev. of *Rejected Addresses* 445). Henham goes over-the-top most obviously when he has eyes hanging from a head "at the end of long strings" and a tongue fallen from "lips, vibrating like a spring" (289). But this horror is part of the Gothic genre's prototypical mix of styles and discourses, both literary and non-literary, lifted from popular theatrical entertainments, evangelical pulpit oratory, exaggerations of exotic fauna and flora in Britain's far-flung empire, myths, legends, and even travel guides like that of the *Western Morning News* for Dartmoor, with enough picturesque or sublimely gloomy rocks, trees, and tarns to flesh out a shelf of "Gothics." Henham's landscape in this novel, however, is only an evocative Dartmoor-ish topography not based on any specific geographic location (e.g. *Tenebrae* 11-12).

The novel is also heir to the later impressionistic techniques of Oscar Wilde's *Dorian Gray* and the decadence of Charles Baudelaire, a translator of Poeandauthor of the Symbolist *Les fleurs du mal* (1857) whose art evokes ecstasy and eroticism, ideal love and betrayal, a beauty hidden by darkness and a darkness staining the light. The narrator's insane uncle, rejoicing in his Baudelairean life of alcohol and concoctions of drugs, is equally a sort of comic Dr. Jekyll–he even teaches his nephew to sweeten coffee with arsenic, something no doyen of etiquette has ever suggested (46). He is the narrator's familiar spirit, responsible for demonic possessions since he styles himself "king of the insects," which is to say, Beelzebub, the king or lord (*Beel*) of the flies (*zebub*, a generic term for insects including flies), another name for Satan. This may be an early lampooning of Henham's clerical uncle with whom the young boy lived–all the vices the righteous vicar abhorred are chalked up to this toadying uncle. For Henham, such psychic opposites as Puritanical religiosity and all-licensed depravity are both blights to the soul. Taking his cue from those innovators who regenerated a decades-dominant Romanticism, Henham composes a horrifying scenario–the schizoid anarchy of a rational malevolent mind torn apart by its insane subconscious guilt. Henham might or might not have been aware of his multiple subtexts; but *Tenebrae* overtly deals with the first-person narrator's self-justifications and self-deceptions. What he repressively cannot admit to be the truth defines his madness as his self splits off from its moral environment. *Tenebrae*, then, becomes something more than mere literary sensationalism of only historical interest.

Although in reality,*Tenebrae* is the offspring of earlier Gothic and Symbolist traditions, Henham disguises a late Victorian cultural uncertainty and irresolution behind his diverse mix of sources. Thus the novel's overlaying appeal to popular taste and intended commercial success is not in conflict with its artistic design because both its hold on the popular imagination and its covert self-expression are outcomes of the same anxieties. The emotions in Henham's scenes are classically paranoid-schizoid, allowing his readers to imagine with cathartic intensity the traumas of real life crises and fears through a fictionalized reality. But if the "turbid lineaments" of Henham's own struggles with his inhibited personality are disguised in Gothic images and conventions, which life events produced which passages? His morbidity and "bewildering mysticism" in several of these early novels might suggest a psychological distress stemming from his orphaning, his troubled relationship with his clerical uncle, his struggle with his health, or possibly a sexual angst produced by a childhood of severe religious repression. *Tenebrae*'s narrator "lusting . . . to kill" (198) suggests a dangerously repressed sexuality–not Henham's actual impulse here but his fittingly artistic sublimation of those inhibitions by a description of the narrator's acting out.

Part I ("The Foreshadowing") describes the protagonist's alienation from his once loved younger brother who has taken his girlfriend away from him–as he says, "seduced her affections" (96). Hints by his old nurse and the mad uncle are inescapably confirmed when he voyeuristically spies upon the lovers. He even interrogates his visual evidence by comparison to a literary anecdote of misunderstood motives, only to reflect that he had overheard their love-making also. Whereas the elder brother's world grows dark, mad, and filled with hate, the younger's appears sane and contented. A key parallel in this novel's structure is the theme of contrasting fraternal brothers from the biblical tale of

Cain and Able, especially the extra-biblical interpretation in the Midrash that identifies the real motive for murder as jealousy over a desirable woman. The narrator's palm-print lifeline is a foreshadowing of the mark of Cain that afterwards appears as blood upon his forehead. Another echo in *Tenebrae* comes from Shakespeare's *The Winter's Tale* (1611) in which King Leontes becomes possessed with jealousy, convinced that his childhood friend, King Polixenes, has seduced his wifeHermione: "I have drunk, and seen the spider" (2.1.45). Polixenes had recalled the age of innocence when he and Leontes were boys, pure even from original sin. Suddenly, the spider in the cup, sexual jealousy, corrupts that deep affection. Henham, it is true, gives his narrator's "spider" a genuine foundation–"My brother had been guilty of vile treachery, and therefore I hated him. The woman abused me, while sharing in my brother's deceit"(108)–but in both works obsessive jealousy over which reason has no sway begets the spider-bitten soul.

In Henham's tale, the traditional polarities of good and evil or darkness and light overlap in this context of sexual rivalry. The elder brother is wealthy, introverted, nervous, and violently envious of his handsome but poor younger brother, who is too weak to confess honestly to his older sibling his sexual conquest. The woman's excuse that her new lover didn't want to give his brother "pain" (300) rings hollow. Both brothers, after all, are flawed–insecure and uncertain of their identities, sharing a dark symbiosis of love now turned to deceit and hate: "We shared, as it were, the same heart, the same mind, equal portions of the same soul. Only the law of Nature compelled us to pass through life beneath the identity of separate bodies" (13). For that reason, he explains: "Had I not loved you so greatly in the past, the hatred of the present had been less" (87). With an allusion from William Blake's "The Sick Rose," the older brother gives the girl roses from which his phobia–a spider–creeps forth (105). The "dark secret love" of a guilty romance has penetrated and sickened what should have been an open and trusting affection, destroying innocence, beauty, life. Not long before the fratricide, the narrator destroys in the fireplace a framed picture with his and his brother's photographs: "I had burnt my own portraiture with his; in figuratively destroying him, I had inflicted a like injury upon myself" (76). The narrator thereafter mutilates and throws his younger brother from a cliff onto the sea rocks: "Physically and mentally my brother was far weaker than myself. . . . With my small knife I stabbed the eyes which had looked into hers, the lips which had been pressed upon hers, the hand which had fondled her, even the heart which had throbbed for her" (18, 122). He then scrambles down to weight his body with stones. In a last ghoulishly convulsive gesture, the victim thrashes out at the narrator–seemingly anticipating such later famous cinematic moments as that in Henri-Georges Clouzot's movie *Diabolique* where Simone Signoret pops out of the bath, subsequently "quoted" in numerous other film endings, such as Adrian Lyne's *Fatal Attraction*.

In Part II, "The Under-shadow," Henham creates a neologism formed by analogy with "overshadow," implying not the penumbra created from the sun's light above but the spider's "darkness visible" (Milton) from hell. The title of Henham's novel is the Latin noun, singular or plural, meaning "shadows" or "darkness"–and also "gloom," "blindness," "night," "death." He adapts his phrase, "*Ave, Tenebrae! Ego moriturus vos saluto*" (263) from Suetonius's *Lives of the Caesars* (AD 121) in which combatants fated to die once addressed the emperor Claudius: "Hail, Emperor, those who are about to die salute you." Henham's version is in the first person: "Hail, Darkness! I who am about to die salute you." He was doubtless aware of its ironic pagan contrast to the invocation of darkness in the Catholic and Anglican services during Holy Week at which the crucifixion is commemorated by a gradual extinguishing of candles: "Hail, darkness, as I walk towards you. . . . " After the darkness of betrayal, suffering, and death, Christ brings redemption connoted by the light of Easter morning. In Henham's novel, darkness becomes a personified horror: a spider in an all-but-haunted house mirrors a fantasy love that, unrequited, exacerbates the vengeance of a dangerously egocentric madman. The ordinary spider in the garden is described by the mad uncle as "the largest I have seen for a long time. His great body is covered thickly with long hairs. Then there is the cross. You cannot help seeing it. It is a white cross, and very distinct" (6). Henham here is thinking of the common garden "diadem" or "cross spider" (*Araneus diadematus*) with five or more large white dots in the shape of a cross. But by the end of the narrative it has become an infernal apotheosis the size of a bear with a human face, the dark double of the narrator and also a *diabolous ex machina*, Lucifer himself as the anti-Christ. The predecessor to Henham's vampirish spider is found in Bertram Mitford's classic *Sign of the Spider* (1896) that may have provided him with this idea of a bear-sized human-faced spider (164, 258). Both Mitford and Henham's spiders also incorporate features of the death's head spider (*Eriophora ravilla*), the crab spider (*Misumenoides formosipes*), the skull spider (*Pholcus phalangioides*), and the jumping spider (*Phidippus audax*).

The narrator believes in an ethereal "Presence" flowing around him, out of which his growing guilt slowly takes its material arachnid incarnation. Following the foreshadowing of vengeance in the form of an everyday spiderin the first part, the ghostly "under-shadow" of Part II begins as a black "scar" (221) on the wall that feeds fat on crime and guilt to become the embodied vampiric spider, the "living substance of a crime" (256). The narrator exclaims in Poe-like hysteria: "'There–huge and horrible in the centre of the wall. Its body is like ebony, except for the silver cross. . . . Why does it bear that mark? Such a sign they erect over graves'" (282-283). He then recalls the Lord stigmatized Cain: "'It was the mark of the white cross upon the black soul. That was the mark set upon the forehead of Cain'" (283). From a sexual point of view, spiders symbolize the core fantasies and conflicts from various developmental levels; they emblematize feelings of repulsion and anxiety, of being "caught in the web" of desires, emotions, and personal feelings of dependence and need. When an intensely ambivalent person battles against a break with reality, the spider often emerges as a symbol of the feared and deeply repressed aspects both of the self's potentially psychotic core and of the vampire woman who debilitates and drains her prey. Here the narrator's *soi-disant* fiancée, suspecting he has murdered his brother, pretends to love him and only marries him to revenge herself on him: "I had resolved to hang over you, like the vampire, the fury, until you should . . . sink to your damnation by the frenzied act of the suicide" (301). His marriage to her is grotesquely consummated in his hallucination of the spider that drops from the ceiling onto his face like a massy *vagina dentata* (235).

As the protagonist visualizes the spider inexorably advancing to destroy him, his wife enters pursued by the crazy uncle. By now the spider has become a deeply metaphorical image that combines the storm of the older brother's anger, his younger brother's deceit, and the wife's revenge–murder, deceit, revenge are the spiders he sees in the poisoned cup. The uncle's arsenic, laudanum, opium, nicotine, and alcohol are their literal complements. Despite foreshadowing and such analogues as his burned photograph or his uncle's report of two spiders fighting, "the smaller one wanted to get away . . . but the larger one—he was cowardly, nephew—ran up behind, and attacked him" (138), the narrator fails to see what has been adumbrated from the beginning. All along he had seen the spider as the Other–as the revenge of his ghostly brother, or of the woman, or of his sin itself in a fantastic bestial shape: "Each was a child of that Shadow which Crime had made" (220). But what about himself, not the sin but the *sinner*? The true spider appeared when he looked at himself in the mirror: "A more hideous face surely had never passed into life from Nature's mould, for the features were pinched and diabolic, the lips a twisted blue line, the mad eyes were filled with blood. But presently I understood that I was gazing upon myself" (219). He reluctantly admits: "The Lord had set a mark upon Cain–the mark of the Shadow, the mark of the eternally damned. And I was Cain" (230). The venomous wife provides a knife to entice her husband into suicide to escape further agony. After the uncle leaps to his death possessed by the evil spirits of his "new mixture" (285), the narrator is discovered–with an echo here from *The Picture of Dorian Gray*–dead with his wife's knife in his heart, fulfilling Friedrich Nietzsche's psychological dictum that decadent souls express themselves most creatively in their own self-destruction.

CHAPTER 3

JOHN TREVENA

About 1895, after his four-year stint in Canada, Henham returned to England, at first very near starvation trying to support himself in London, then living with his uncle and aunt at Wallingford, Berkshire (after 1974 known as Oxfordshire). Around this time he traveled on several occasions to the Swiss-Italian Alps "seeking health and flowers," as he recalls in his volume which is a botanical treatise, a collection of pen-portraits of Italian mountain figures, and a heavily edited memoir (*Adventures* 29). Henham envisions life as beauty and suffering within a fearfully brief interval. He devotes a good bit of chapter six to a young girl called Paolina, who is situated among a pasture of wild flowers in a landscape very much like William Wordsworth's "Highland Lass." Standing under a lowering sky that heightens the color saturation of the field flowers, Paolina, like the wild flowers she brings to the Madonna in church, will be "swept down by the scythe" (80). Her devotion does not protect her from the blade of time. Only the beauty of the flowers allows humanity fleetingly to forget its sorrows, horrors, and the Mark of the Shadow. A story also is told to Trevena by a pedlar–a "funny" true story–of a popular village lunatic whose practical jokes finally get out of hand as the hilarious turns into grotesque cruelty. Where does the amusement stop and the horror begin? This is not unrelated to exquisite beauty in a life suspended between calamities of irremediable loss.

In 1901, single and past thirty, Henham is living with his aunt, widowed in 1900. For "adventures" among the botanically "wild," Trevena walked, studied plants, and gardened. By 1903, his tuberculosis had become active and he went into treatment in the area of Belstone (called Lew in *Pixy in Petticoats*) between Okehampton and the village of Sticklepath. F.T. Cooper noted that "ill-health has been his lot for the greater part" of the first four decades of his life, and:

> he finally learned that the smoky, tainted air of English towns acted upon him as a slow poison. Dartmoor, with its high alti-

> tudes, its level, wind-swept stretches, offered a chance for recovery; and there, for several years, John Trevena has been living in voluntary exile in a little isolated cabin, doing all of the manual work, unaided, drawing in, day by day, deep draughts of health, in his endless wanderings over the moors, and finding an inexhaustible source of entertainment in studying the curiously warped and stunted types of humanity produced by nature's struggle for survival. (325)

According to Martin, this "turning-point in his career as an author came when he was unexpectedly left a small legacy by a relative, which enabled him to stop writing for a time and consider his position. Doctors informed him that his health was seriously affected, that he was in fact a consumptive. So he came to live for a time on Dartmoor and the life there brought about a decided improvement, though it could not effect a cure" (325). In 1914 Trevena recalled with a certain wit:

> During the greater part of life I have been a dweller in high places. Some men are born with a love for mountains, other have the fondness thrust upon them. For my own part I have been always of Dr. Johnson's opinion, that nobody would live outside London unless compelled to do so; and certainly the time when I watched the flow of life along Great Russell Street was the happiest period of all. I had been preparing myself for journalism by studying, unwisely I now think, the style of De Quincey and Addison . . . But long before I could form any style whatever, a smoke barrier was set up between the career of journalism and myself; and I was sent to try sea air, and to wander in lonely places. (*Adventures* 13)

Trevena had made an even more revealing statement as reported in the *Writer* (1915):

> At the age of sixteen I was attacked by disease, and the disease remained with me until, in my thirty-sixth year, I shook it off upon Dartmoor, a region for which I have little affection, despite my books. Four early years I spent in Canada, and upon returning to London I was reduced to something uncomfortably like starvation, until certain stern, Puritanical relatives gave me a home. Under the rigorous treatment I received there—they looked upon literature as a form of idleness and novel-writing as one of the deadly sins; according to their lights, placing every possible impediment in my way—my

> health broke down entirely. At the same time Providence sent me an unexpected legacy of four hundred pounds. I went to live in the Italian Alps, but grew rapidly worse, so I came back to England; was sent by a doctor to Bournemouth, where I entered the last stage; finally was carried to Dartmoor, where I recovered. With few pounds left I took a cottage, and there made my final throw against fate by writing 'A Pixy in Petticoats.' If it failed I was done for. While awaiting publication I lived by selling a few engravings. The book was not a great success, but it was enough to set me upon my feet. ("John Trevena" 105-106)

In *Heather,* the protagonist George received £500 from his aunt as an advance on a future legacy; Trevena's "stern, Puritanical relatives" would be an unusual source, even though his aunt Millicent had been widowed recently in 1900.As John Burrough had been in *Pixy*, Henham too was sent to Dartmoor to "rebuild his lungs" (10). Théophile Tanguy, who explored Trevena's various Dartmoor domiciles a dozen years after his death, claims he took up residence in a corrugated-iron-roofed hillside cottage south of Belstone called "Pixies' Hut" where the windows opened on the untainted air from the moors and Cawsand Beacon, overlooking at a distance the Taw River in Belstone cleave. His information is derived from "research on the ground, December 1960," among the still-extant local oldsters (6).

By now Trevena had about a half dozen novels and even more short stories to his credit, all published under his name of Ernest Henham. Then in 1906 he brought out his next novel anonymously, *A Pixy in Petticoats*, with a Dartmoor background. *Pixy* is the story of a man like Henham himself living on Dartmoor–companionless save for his cat–until the tantalizingly embodied pixy, Beatrice Pentreath, comes into his life. The *Writer* here quotes J. Walter Smith, London correspondent of the *Boston Evening Transcript*:

> "It is one thing, however, to make a literary success, and another to pay for it," says J. Walter Smith, in the Boston Transcript. "Trevena paid for his in an unexpected way. His 'Pixy,' be it known, was founded upon a real person—in fact, every character in the book, except Burrough, the hero, was real. When Trevena's villagers found out the truth—that their doings and sayings had been published to the world, excite-

> ment grew to indignation. Trevena's life was actually threatened, and he made a hasty exit to another part of Dartmoor. Once when taking a quiet walk on the moor, so he himself says, a rifle bullet whizzed past his head, and he never learned who fired it. At that time he was doing his literary work in a secluded cottage on the top of a hill, commanding a wonderful view of the Tors which figure often in his stories. 'There I lived,' he said some years ago, in reply to a request for information about himself, 'absolutely alone with my dogs, doing my own cooking and housework for months together. Often I did not speak to any one for over a week. I seemed to be a source of some terror to the nearest village, as the people, who are still superstitious, regarded me as a magician, practising the black arts in solitude.' Trevena's books show how thoroughly he has studied the Dartmoor folk. One feels the touch of truth in all he writes. This is not surprising when one knows that nearly all his characters are painted from the life, and that for years, while he has been fighting for his very physical existence amongst the heather and granite which he knows so well, he has been filling his brain with a mass of Dartmoor folk-lore and fact, the value and nature of which cannot be estimated until Trevena has written his last book." (106)

Pixies' Hut today still stands adjacent to a larger house called at that time "the Sanatorium" with a half dozen or more patients in residence, asdescribed in chapter two of *Heather*.

Undoubtedly this is the cottage to which Henham was "carried," but it is not the same as the one on the hilltop described in *Pixy* as "the little cottage with the tin roof at the end of the gorge" (76)."About this time," writes Brian Le Messurier, "a Dr. Gwynn was using other cottages in the hamlet as a 'sanatorium' in which he lodged his consumptive patients, so it is possible that Henham was also in his care" (Messurier 6). This would be Neville Claude Gwynn, physician and surgeon in Tawcroft and Belstone, Devon, who died in 1945. The name of the sanatorium structure today is "Birchy Lake," whether recently adopted for this property or not is unknown; in 2012 it was for rent as a holiday cottage. Although Trevena certainly had preferred the urban bustle of Great Russell Street, now he "communicated little with the outside world, sometimes not speaking to anyone for over a week. He spent his time writing or walking over the Moor and the surrounding countryside with his dogs, talking to himself as he went and wearing unconventional clothes" (6). He wrote the majority of his best novels against the village background of this Dartmoor area which he grew to admire: "Sticklepath, most happily named of villages, for its path or road runs beside the Taw river, with its numerous stickles, or little falls, which turn five water-wheels amid dripping ferns and flowering grasses and rhododendrons of pink and scarlet" (*Arminel* 5).

But though *Pixy* was anonymous, its characters, as noted, were anything but unrecognized. Théophile Tanguy reports from conversations "with Mrs. Pearse and other villagers, Sticklepath, April 1961":

> Some of the oldest inhabitants in Belstone still remember quite well the tall, gaunt figure roaming about the village and walking over the moors. They remember too the uproar created by the publication of *A Pixy in Petticoats*, and the subsequent "mobilisation" of the villagers under the leadership of William Ellis [the prototype of Willum Cobbledick], the "scholar" and his mother Ann . . . in order to make "Mr. Anon" (the book was published anonymously) pay damages for the libels he had perpetrated. And William Ellis's famous remarks were popular at the time in Belstone and the neighbourhood: "You know the man Henham 'ee wrote a buke all about us proper wicked. Me and Dr. Young into Okehampton, us is going to write all about 'ee. There is plenty there 'ee wouldn't like people to know." (7)

Brian Le Messurier,the local historian, reports: "My own copy of 'Arminel,' bought for a shilling in a second-hand bookshop four years ago, contains a sheet of notepaper in the handwriting of the original owner identifying the characters of the book as real Spreyton and South Tawton inhabitants. This shows how much he used actual people in his novels" (6). According to local inhabitants, not only was Willum Cobbledick a literal person, but Ann his mother in reality did milk her cow in the middle of the road. Even their thatched home still stands in Belstone village–the "Lew" of both *Pixy* and *The Dartmoor House that Jack Built* (1909). Other characters in *Pixy* also have known historical counterparts: Wannell who never had a bath was William Brock, his identification confirmed a half century ago by his grandson who was still living in Belstone. This real-life eccentric crops up again in the hilarious description of Jack Zaple's first bath in *Arminel* (211-212). The Belstone rectory stood in the middle of Lew village, exactly as described in *Pixy*, with garden and gate where old Yeoland ogled the girls. Also William Redaway, landlord of the Tors Hotel, became personified in the novel as Eastaway of the Plume of Feathers pub, where likewise William Westaway is presented as Kellaway, Sam Parr as Wollacott, and Belstone's drunken rector Luke, whom Ellis had to help back home every evening, probably supplied the *donnée* for Griffey the preacher. Luke's particular failing may also reappear in *Granite* broadly reincarnated both in Hosken, the croquet-playing the vicar, and in Spiller his curate.

Then in 1907 with the publication of *Arminel of the West*, following*A Pixy in Petticoats*, Henham introduced his pen name "John Trevena"although his neighbors continued to know him as Mr. Henham. Frederic Cooper's overview makes no mention of any prior "Henham" works and cites *A Pixy in Petticoats* as his first novel. (Its 1908 reprinting was afterwards published under his newpseudonym.) Henham chose his Cornish pen nameprobably because he was attracted to the mythic associations of south-western England's history and legends. Up until the middle of the nineteenth century, "Trevena" had been the name of a village on the Atlantic coast of Cornwall in the folklore-rich parish of Tintagel. But in a modern commercializing ploy it changed its name to "Tintagel" to increase tourism. In the 1230s or 1240s, Earl Richard of Cornwall, a son of King John, inspired by the stories associated with the area of King Arthur, Merlin, and also the tragic myth of Tristan and Yseult, erected a gothic fairy-tale castle there, perhaps on the ruins of an earlier fortification. Earl Rich-ardbelieved this had been the location of Arthur's court because the Welsh cleric and chronicler Geoffrey of Monmouth had said so. Geoffrey's *Historia Regum Britanniae* (c. 1136) was the first to mention a castle of "Tintagol"; later, in Layamon's *Bruit* (c.1190-1215) it was spelled "Tintaieol." In Geoffrey's account, the Duke of Cornwall when he went to war had placed his wife, who "in beauty did surpass all the other dames of the whole of Britain, . . . in the Castle of Tintagol on the seacoast" (Monmouth 216-217). Merlin disguised the infatuated Uther Pendragon as her husband, who thus fathered King Arthur by her. Thomas Malory's *Le Morte*

D'Arthur, first published by William Caxton in 1485, has proved the most potent retelling of the legend. Much more recently, Alfred Tennyson, who in 1848 visited Tintagel for his first but not the last time, had sat in the rain and viewed the "old castle darkening in the gloom" (Huckel 171); it became the setting for his Arthurian cycle, *Idylls of the King*.

Myrtle Henry, quoting indirectly from a Trevena letter, comments: "The writer, because of his fondness for the Cornish Coast, took his *nom de plume* from a little village beside Tintagel, with the result, he adds, that his novels have been more popular in Cornwall than elsewhere. The Cornish, 'a clannish folk,' accepted him as one of themselves. He has returned their affection. He loves the Cornish, the people of 'good hearts' and 'proud blood'" (20)–just the opposite, one may observe, of his experience with the distrustful locals on Dartmoor whom he ridiculed as stupid and slovenly. Although "John Trevena" primarily resided in Dartmoor where his West Country novels largely are set, his pseudonym appears to be another "materialization" of the land, deriving from the Cornish: *Tre war Venydh*. In Cornish,*Tre* means "farm or dwelling; *war* translates as "on"; and *venydh* is "a hill." Cornish, which is linguistically quite unlike English, derived from the Celtic of ancient Gaul and pre-Roman Britain, and this doubtless enhanced its fascination for Trevena. But one is tempted to suggest further that Henham's adoption of this pseudonym is akin to Hardy's use of "Wessex"–an elision for the ancient "West Saxon" kingdoms of England–to identify his home county of Dorset and its surrounding southwest areas. Each author's place name is firmly fixed in a landscape hallowed byantique figures and doings, at odds with their own industrial century.

Of course, Trevena's decision, as he tells Myrtle Henry (29, 37n), was also related to a (misguided?) sense that his earlier historical and fantastic romances were novice productions and that by starting anew they would remain unknown or be forgotten. Like Cooper's essay, the *Who's Who* entries for Trevena from 1928–1944 begin his list of publications with the 1906 *Pixy*, citing by title only the "Trevena" novels. Henham told one interviewer that those earlier works were by "an obscure and ill-balanced scribbler, whose difficulties were insurmountable" ("John Trevena" 105). Paul Jordan-Smith characterized his earlier novels as "too melodramatic" (*Times* IV9). "It is easy," Trevena observed, "to take the pen but hard to control it. . . . We writers under the stress of work, irritation, or infirmity are apt to think carelessly and to set down many a phrase which later we deplore. Even the sentence which the brain wishes to express may reach the hand in another form, and be twisted by the demon in the pen into a flat denial of the truth" (*Adventures* 157).

One cannot help feeling that some further personal influence may have been at play as well, perhaps a romantic companion's disapproval of lurid Gothic elements. In *Heather,* George describes to Bubo, his one-legged owl, a novel "they" wrote as "a sort of catch-money thing, and it was vilely well done, for you and I can turn out tolerable stuff when the pinch comes; but it was dirty, filthy, a lustful thing; . . .we remembered the saying of a man who had made a success of his life, though perhaps he never took the trouble to look at his hands very closely, 'My boy,' he said, 'if you want to make money at this writing game, write fornication'" (302). George and Bubo then withdraw this manuscript after its acceptance for the sake of the girl George loves: "We didn't know what love was, and how absolutely pure it can be. Not a matter of blood and lust, Bubo; not at all. Not a matter of this secret or that secret and shame between; but a soul, a personality, eyes, hair, nose, dimples, a little movement, a hand at rest on your arm, two small feet at your fireside, a certain manner that is nowhere else–see what a lot of beautiful things against the one that is base" (302). At any rate, Henham's new pen-name was no mere evolution in his career but a real *revolution.*

Sources that Trevena consulted for historical and other background data for his new Dartmoor fiction included J.D. Prickman, "West Country Wit and Humor" (1898), John L.W. Page, "Pixies" (1892), and Robert Hunt's *Popular Romances of the West of England* (1865). One principal published source is clearly an anonymous essay in *The Quarterly Review* cited in the volume contents as a critique of several works but in its running head as "The Pleasant Land of Devon" (1894). Trevena relied on several interesting examples in this essay for the factual underlayment of his imaginative recreation of Dartmoor's land and history:

In any survey of the County of Devon, the first object which attracts the attention is the great central waste, known as the Forest of Dartmoor. . . . It is thus described by Risdon, writing about the year 1630, and two centuries and a half have effected little change in its external aspect:–

"Between the North and the South Hams (for that is the ancient name) there lieth a chain of hills consisting of a blackish earth, both rocky and heathy, called by a borrowed name of its barrenness *Dartmoor*; richer in its bowels than in the face thereof, yielding tin and turf, which to save for fuel, you would wonder to see how busy the bye-dwellers be at some seasons of the year, whose tops and torrs are in the winter often covered with a white cap, but in the summer the bordering neighbours bring great herds of cattle and flocks of sheep to pasture there. From these hills, or rather mountains, the mother of many rivers, the land declineth either way; witness their divers courses: some of which disburthen themselves into the British ocean; others, by long wandering, seek the Severn sea."

Next we have a paragraph that anticipates Trevena's caustic attitude towards the natives:

It is the struggle with a niggard soil and a rigorous climate that has given the Highlanders of Devon those qualities of thrift and industry which have formed so fine a blend with their more somnolent, but yet not less enterprising, brethren of the plains. Something, too, of the feudal spirit still lingers among the tenants of the Duchy. Their service, indeed, consists in little else than assisting at the "drifts" in which the horned cattle and ponies are collected, branded, and the "strays" returned to their owners. Sheep-stealing had been in vogue until recent times since the days of the Gubbings, who levied blackmail on the southern fringe of the moor, and where "wealth," as [Thomas] Fuller says [in The *Worthies of England*, 1662], "consisted in other men's goods.". . .

The tenants of the Duchy have had lenient landlords; but if scant "service" has been required of them, they have none the less clung tenaciously to their own privileges of mining, turbary, and quarrying. They have, too, like others in similar circumstances, experienced the necessity of supplementing their resources at the expense of others. They have been known to "straighten" a boundary wall at the cost of their distant landlord, and have helped themselves freely to whatever their stony wilderness afforded. Their creed is that whatever God placed in the country was meant for their use.

Because of these "privileges" (turbary is the right to cut peat for fuel) the "tenants" of the Duchy are known as "commoners," so called because they have joint rights in Dartmoor's common moorland.

The *Quarterly* author makes the point that the land appeals to the imagination for several reasons, including its neolithic and Roman past, its quaint superstitions, and its pagan customs. Of the prehistoric "huts and hut-circles" of herdsmen and miners, the author writes:

> If anything were needed to enhance the solemnity with which Nature has invested the weird waste of Dartmoor, it would be found in the footprints left by the races which once inhabited it: . . . Open though their dwellings now are to the sky, they were presumably once closed by materials which have proved less durable than their sides, and when chinked with turf would afford an efficient protection from the weather. The walled enclosures known as "pounds" served a like purpose for the cattle, and as a refuge for the tribesmen in the event of a sudden foray. . . . In the wider reaches [of rivers] rough granite blocks are employed as piers to support the roadway, but the smaller streams are spanned by a single gigantic slab of granite. . . .No one can wander far through the West without coming on traces of the supernatural life with which it once was peopled. . . :–
>
> "Pixyland is a shadowy realm, somewhere beneath the bogs, down which the pixies vanish at the approach of dawn, or when weary of dancing on the smoother pieces of turf. Hence the pixy king, who there holds court, despatches his messengers to visit the people of upper earth, who, by reason of their uncanny tricks, entertain for the little folk considerable awe."
>
> The pixies, however, when kindly treated, are like their Northern brethren, assiduous in their kindly offices. . . .The superstitious dread, however, which has preserved the barrows, has not been equally efficacious in protecting the ancient relics. "*Quod non fecerunt barbari, fecere Barberini*"is not applicable to Rome alone["What the barbarians did not do, the Barberini <Roman nobility of the Renaissance>did"]. The Dartmoor farmer has laid sacrilegious hands

> on many a reverend stone, which centuries had spared. With scant veneration or care for archæology, he pillages the nearest "avenue" or "pound" to build the wall of his "new-take"–Pagan or Christian, it is all one to him; and he selects the shaft of a cross or the doorpost of a hut-circle, with equal indifference, to hang his gate. (414-436)

One's first impulse is to say Trevena borrowed too liberally, but on reflection one can appreciate the integration of his imagination with the tethers of historical detail. Cold fact rises to the level of living symbol; symbol, however, never overwhelms truth to life. As the pre-modern (neolithic in some instances) superstitions and customs of Trevena's folk come into contact with an emergent modernity, the conflict is both farcical and nostalgic, such as Peter Tavy's effort to rig his Bronze Age hut with electric lights or Mary Tavy's first train ridein *Furze the Cruel.*

Around 1908, Trevena moved an inconsequential but tortuous distance and built "Pixies' Garden," an isolated hill-top house above Ramsley Corner in South Zeal. Since Trevena had been in the Alps at the May 1906 opening of the Simplon Tunnel and afterwards (*Adventures*94), his choice of Dartmoor as the permanent recourse for his chronic condition seems to havecoincided with his decision to build "Pixies' Garden." Galbraith, a reviewer, reportedthat year: "A few days ago Mr. Trevena wrote me a letter giving some information about his literary plans, which are at present uncertain because Mr. Trevena is–to use his own words–'a writer whose mind does not work unless I have a pen in my hand. I am preparing, however,' says he, 'to write this Summer a sequel to my first book, 'A Pixy in Petticoats,' the writing of which got me into trouble with the commoners. This will be quite a light book, and much of the fun of it will consist in the fact that I shall caricature myself'" (Galbraith BR402). Decades later, Trevena recalled in similar words that *Pixy* "'got me into trouble with the commoners. . . . I was building at the time and greatly plagued by the natives who detested me, so I held them up to ridicule and in order to be fair ridiculed myself as well'" (Henry 22). Seemingly, then, his self-caricature occurred in both these novels, in *Pixy* as well as in *The Dartmoor House That Jack Built* which opens with Mrs. Cobbledick carrying a staff, looking for a man who "had insulted her son Willum" (1). The townsfolk, of course, suspected Henham "wur afraid to put his rightful name to the buke" to avoid being thrown into a bog by those who felt abusively portrayed (16).

Tanguy observes that the exact date of Trevena's move to Pixies' Garden has not been established, "but several people in South Zeal still remember Trevena walking down to the village and inviting the commoners to drink at his expense while he talked with them in their own dialect–this while studying their way of life and their 'crooked' way of thinking. A favourite maxim among the villagers at this time was: 'Don't say tu much or ye'll be put in a buke'" (8; *Dartmoor House* 139). His actual house, the construction of which is narrated in the novel,is a large two-level structure of concrete blocks faced with a wooden frame, the front wall accommodating twenty-eight windows overlooking an abandoned copper mine at the foot of Ramsley Hill opposite and, downwards to the north, the village of South Zeal. We are told that "in the garden he planted trees and shrubs which still grow in splendid profusion; but here, as at Belstone, he kept to himself, and was regarded with suspicion by the people of South Zeal. . . . Even the girl who delivered the bread never dared to approach his house, but left it some distance away for Trevena to collect" (Messurier 6).

About this time–in 1909 after *Arminel*,*Furze*, and *Heather*-had appeared–the recently organized publishing house of Moffat, Yard & Company gave a supplementary sketch of Trevena in the first issue of its trade circular, "Books and Authors." Though generally unknown, this account together with the essay in the *Writer* may be the most comprehensive biographical profiles extant for Trevena's optimally creative years. A few of these sentences had appeared earlier in "Among the Authors"(22); then substantially later more extensive extracts from J. Walter Smith's original notes appeared in "John Trevena"(105-106). But as reported in the *Boston Evening Transcript*,Moffat, Yard described his novels as:

> rapidly bringing him an international repute. We quote the substance of the sketch: "Mr. Trevena is a bachelor, still on the right side of forty, and passes a very secluded country existence, not leaving Dartmoor more than two or three weeks throughout the year. He is not physically strong, and is thus completely barred from the life of the town, which is, however, no great hardship. His recreations are simply walking,

> gardening and observing Nature and his fellow-creatures. He is a devoted lover of animals, especially dogs; indeed, he confesses to being a dog-fool. His knowledge of Dartmoor is probably unique. He has lived on the moor for years, mixing with the commoners, studying them closely, talking to them in their own dialect, and perhaps not speaking to any of his own class for months. He is a commoner. All other writers have described Dartmoor and its people from the impressions gained by a few short summer visits. Whatever these may be worth, his pictures are true, his incidents actual ones, and this has been somewhat unfortunate for him. His first book raised a regular storm in the village of its origin; his life even was threatened, and he had to fly in rather an undignified fashion. Last September, while walking on the moor, a rifle bullet whistled past his head, and he never found out who fired it. When working he often retires to a lonely little cottage on the top of a hill with a fine view of the tors. There he lives absolutely alone with his dogs, doing his own cooking and housework for months together. Often he does not speak to anyone for over a week. He seems to be a source of some terror to the nearest village, as the people, who are still superstitious, regard him as a magician. He has one peculiarity, which it may be worth while to mention, and that is, he never reads a modern book. He cannot see how any novelist can hope to be original if he reads the works of his contemporaries. English critics are fond of comparing him to Thomas Hardy, or to Zola; but as he has not read anything that these authors have written, the resemblance must be either accidental, or perhaps it only exists in the imagination. He has a good classical library; he reads Latin, Greek and Italian, and studies the newspapers carefully, for it is there the life of a country and real human nature may be found. 'My aim above all,' writes Mr. Trevena, 'is to preach, not so much kindliness, as ordinary justice towards animals; and to remind men and women that they are animals, too.'" (Edgett, 1909:7)

Of course, newspapers certainly did contain book reviews; but one should not swallow his admitted"peculiarity" too unreservedly;Trevena mentions "Glancing up at my bookcase, as I write, my eye falls upon a long row"–of Tauchnitz novels, inexpensive copyright editions (*Adventure* 37). When Arthur Symons called Walter Pater's attention to Olive Schreiner's feminist novel, *The Story of an African Farm* (1883), Pater told him that he probably would never read it; he felt himself too susceptible to distracting influences. But had Trevena not felt so insecure–about losing his originality by reading novels of his peers or about the unsettling possibility of being at a disadvantage facing the competition–and instead fed his imagination with contemporary topics and techniques, he might have recognized possibilities in the emerging psychological novel and outspokenly capitalized on his commanding lead in that genre.

Given Trevena's interest in representing Dartmoor's natural environment and its social life, the local figures treated ethnographically like "savages" continued to recognize themselves in successive books. F.T. Cooper notes that it is not surprising that Trevena's affinity for "the land which has given him back his health . . . should be mirrored back in his books . . . [and] that the people of the moors would go into his books just as he sees them, with an uncompromising literalness of detail that might well give offense and that, as a matter of fact, has once at least so far antagonized his neighbors that he was forced to change his residence with undignified haste, and find lodgment in a new and distant locality" (326). One presumes this is the "undignified" occurrence to which Moffat, Yard also alluded; and it sounds very much like the same event described by Tanguy from "conversation with villagers of Morchard Bishop and Blackdog, December 1960," relating to Trevena's "sudden disappearance from his cottage, one stormy night, never to return. No-one knew exactly why this flight took place and, even to-day, it remains an impenetrable mystery. When he left South Zeal, Trevena probably settled down at Blackdog near Morchard Bishop where it has been impossible to trace him with certainty. He is likely to have lived there under the name of Engart or Ingart as a lodger, but his wife was not with him, and he spent most of his time walking with his dogs" (9). Yet since Trevena had just moved into his new South Zeal house, one presumes, given the size of its construction and extensive landscaping, that the flight must have been earlier*to* South Zeal *after* he had been shot at, or otherwise occurred at some much later date.

Trevena indirectly comments about his career and craft of writing when, in *Pixy,*Burrough explains to Peter the King o' the Cats that "there are three ways of making money with the pen. . . . The first is to write a successful play; the second to produce a novel which everyone reads; and the third to tickle the palate of the public with highly-seasoned serials in halfpenny journals. Number one catches society; number two the middle-class; and number three the 'mostly fools' mentioned by Carlyle."[5] As a classical scholar, Burrough's talents are "not marketable," so he asks his cat for an original idea for fiction, "some new passion, some fresh phase" because "sonnets and essays are things of the past" (63-64). The figure of the poet in *Wintering Hay* whose manuscript is returned with kind words of advice from the publisher also may well be autobiographical. The publisher told Cyril he could not make a living as a poet; he should recast his beautiful imagery in prose (259-260), but Cyril is angered and ignored the advice. In *Moyle Church-Town,* the protagonist observes that "the employments that are open to the gentleman of no profession are few," so short of gambling and horse racing "I must write for the booksellers." A waiter appears who writes non-fiction and hates novels that translate "'the business of life into low and creeping prose. . . . The wings of Minerva are clipped, and her classical gown is fouled with mire. Authorship, sir, is in mighty bad plight at present.'" But he then betrays his egotistical ambition "'to do the History of the World in hexameters and pentameters'" (262-264).

One gathers that Trevena considers the field crowded with dilettantes and poetasters who cannot put a sentence together effectively. That poetry is greatly inferior to fiction for conveying *les mouvements de coeur* was originally, of course, the discovery of Stendhal and Gustave Flaubert. Walter Pater wrote to the young Arthur Symons: "I think the present age an unfavourable one to poets, at least in England. . . . I should say, make prose your principal *métier*, as a man of letters" (Pater, *Letters* 79-80). But it was a unique kind of prose Pater had in mind, if one is to judge from his own sensuous style. Symons noted that Pater, like Baudelaire, "has '*rêvé le miracle d'une prose poétique, musicale sans rhythme et sans rime*'" (Symons 65). If the poetry of law offices and birch bark is dead, and if Trevena will not write the "catch-money" fiction spurned by Bubo, he must undertake to write novels despised by unctuous, unimaginative waiters. Accord-

5. Carlyle, "A parliament speaking through reporters to Buncombe and the twenty-seven millions mostly fools." *Latter Day Pamphlet*, No. 6 (1850).

ingly, one must not read Trevena's fiction fast for incident but slowly for poetic detail, "'the subtle spiritual fire kindling from word to word'" (to return to Symons). Symbolists aside, in Trevena one recognizes the touch of a master–as in his simple, winsomely memorable image of the winter's day as "a little grey yawn between two long nights" (*Heather,* 260).

Of his Dartmoor trilogy of novels, Trevena wrote in a prefatory note to *Furze the Cruel* (1907), the first in the series: "Almost everywhere on Dartmoor are Furze, Heather, and Granite. The Furze seems to suggest Cruelty, the Heather Endurance, and the Granite Strength. The Furze is destroyed by fire, but grows again; the Heather is torn by winds, but blossoms again; the Granite is worn away imperceptibly by the rain. This work is the first of a proposed trilogy, which the author hopes to continue and complete with 'Heather' and 'Granite.'" *Heather* appeared in 1908 and *Granite* in 1909. F.T. Cooper commented: "In these three symbols, he finds typified the dominant traits of the Dartmoor folk, as he has come to know them, perhaps, also, in a broader way, the traits which everywhere, and at all times, have had the largest share in the molding of society and of nations. And in making a trilogy of these three symbols, he seems to be trying to say that the world is not wholly cruel . . . but from the blending of these . . . we get a pretty good presentment of real life" (334). And in 1910, this original moorland trilogy became a quartet when Trevena published *Bracken.* The bracken plant is described biologically by Cooper as "the rank, riotous, rapid-growing fern-plant, sole survivor in England of the carboniferous period, [that] stands as a link with the past, a symbol of the primordial, a reminder of the stability of flora on earth, and of the comparative narrow space that separates the cave man from his brother of to-day" (339). As much as Cooper had loved *Furze*, he detested *Bracken*: "It possesses the dubious distinction of being the most repulsive book that I have read in many years. In *Furze the Cruel*, Mr. Trevena first gave evidence of a tendency to see and picture life symbolically. But *Bracken* is symbolism running amuck, a weird, creepy, madhouse symbolism, suggestive of things in heaven and earth of which it is not good to dream in any man's philosophy" (338).

In the same year as the publication of this fourth novel of spirits and plant-life, an important private event transpired for the author. I shall paraphrase the General Register Office document:

> On 28 July 1910 the union of Ernest George Henham, bachelor, 39 years of age, an author, resident at Pixy's Garden Cottage, Sticklepath, Okehampton, Devon, the son of Thomas Henham, gentleman, deceased, and Selina Rose McDonald, spinster, age 30, resident at 54 Fentiman Road, SW8 Lambeth, daughter of Donald McDonald, florist, deceased, was solemnized by W.B. Chalmers, Curate of the parish Church of St. Mark, St. Mark's Road, Notting Hill, Kensington, London, according to the rites and ceremonies of the Established Church, as witnessed by Millicent Henham (the bridegroom's aunt), Frances Jane Grindley, and Ellen Ward.

The bride Selina, known as Rose, was of Scottish ancestry but born in the province of Prince Edward Island, Canada, in 1870, the youngest of six siblings. Trevena's *Who's Who* entry identifies her as from Dumfries, Scotland, although nine years previous to her marriage the British census reveals she had been living in Northumberland, England. Her true age according to Canadian and British census records should have been listed on the marriage certificate as forty. Searle calls attention to a few sentences in Jerome K. Jerome's autobiography, *My Life and Times*, when Trevena "was a neighbour of ours at Wallingford." This is where Trevena was living with his aunt in 1901: "The woman to whom he was engaged died. But he always spoke of her as if she were living–would talk with her in his study and go long walks with her. He built himself a solitary house high up on Dartmoor. Lived there by himself for a time. And then quite suddenly he married his typist" (Jerome 182).

That Rose's family was Roman Catholic may have prompted Trevena's later remark that "no body of men has been more grievously libelled than the Roman Catholic priesthood"; despite their full share of human flaws, "they compare more than favourably with the clergy of any other creed." Trevena contrasts the comfortable Anglican rector (memories of the Vicar of Streatley) with the austere Catholic priest: "Yet, with all his disadvantages, the Catholic priest appears to stumble less frequently than his

Anglican brother, whom he must not own as such" (*Adventures* 211-212). One recognizes here the symbolism of the literally stumbling Pezzack in *Furze* who, lacking institutional affiliation as a non-conformist minister and depending entirely on his congregants, foolishly placed himself at the mercy of the villainous Pendoggat. Trevena seemingly shared with similarly-minded writers of the early twentieth-century's Catholic Revival–Graham Greene, Evelyn Waugh, G.K. Chesterton and such Anglo-Catholics as T.S. Eliot or C.S. Lewis, each to some degree influenced by the Oxford Movement or the prose and poetry of John Henry Newman–the conviction that contemporary life's malaise of self-indulgence, angst, and guilt lacked necessary historical and traditional spiritual values, although Trevena for his own part found the grace of God neither in Catholicism nor in the Thirty-Nine Articles but in the life of nature. In *Bracken,* Jasper Ramrige declares that "a soul would rather roam beneath these oaks in the beauty of twilight than inhabit the heaven of the churches" (215). Trevena seems to have worked out for himself what one might call a personal non-monotheistic spirituality.

It would indeed be wonderful to have more biographical data from Trevena's life about such details. Martin quotes an opinion of Paul Jordan-Smith that "a full-scale 'analysis'" of Trevena would reveal to us "one of the most painfully interesting figures of this century" (87). Though psychosexual studies of some writers have offered at times powerful insights, Trevena remains one for whom no such biography is likely. To draw the facts of his life from his art is certainly to invert the usual *modus operandi*. Which fictional clergymen are most like his uncle? Which women are like the lost fiancée, which like Rose? Which figures are like himself? Writing of the discreet Walter Pater, Mary Ward had noted that nationally the English "are not fond of direct 'confessions'. . . English feeling, at its best and subtlest, has almost always something elusive in it, something which resents a spectator, and only moves at ease when it has succeeded in interposing some light screen or some obvious mask between it and the public" (134). Henry James had remarked at Pater's death: "I think he has had–will have had–the most exquisite literary fortune: i.e. to have taken it out all, wholly, exclusively, with the pen (the style, the genius), and absolutely not at all with the person. He is the mask without the face, and there isn't in his total superficies a tiny point of vantage for the newspaper to flap its wings on" (James, Lubbock 1:222). So also Trevena.

Eventually, he was "outed" as Henham, first by "E.O.J." in the *Cornhill Booklet* (1914), and then again–twice–by the *New York Times*:

> It is one of the strangest facts in literary history that a man, who had defined his place as a writer of fiction with nine novels or so, published under his own name, should have seen fit, after the Boer War, to begin his career afresh and write a long series of commercially unsuccessful novels under a pseudonym. The novelist who now employs the *nom de guerre*, "John Trevena," and who has ceased to publish fiction under his own name, is a man of middle age with over twenty distinguished volumes to his credit. His fame, like that of Meredith, has been slow in arrival (at least as "John Trevena"), but may be predicted as safely permanent after it comes. Contrary to the general impression, "John Trevena," who lives in retirement in the south of England, is married. He is associated, we may add, in the minds of many, with a great fondness for animals.

Other critics also compared Trevena to George Meredith, and not only because of the public's indifference to their fiction. Meredith's analytical characterizations wrapped in digressions, his profusion of minor figures and rustics depicted without empathy, his inherited transcendentalism at odds with evolutionary facts of life—all this makes such a correlation entirely befitting. Oxenham continues:

> As a young man he travelled widely in the New World, and like so many young Englishmen, struggled for life in the Canadian Northwest. He retains a vivid picture of the Riel Rebellion in Canada in the 80's. . . . Our readers may find that his passion for Nature and his insistence on its blind unyielding influence on human character and fate furnishes a clue to his private personality. . . . He has never published a volume of poems to our knowledge, or written about Dartmoor under his own name. He is not wealthy, seldom sees visitors, and is seen in London only for a day or two, and not oftener than once a year. . . .

> Briefly, these novels are the expression of a passionate feeling for Nature, considered as the sum of human personality and experience, in all its moods–benign and malign, as man is benign and malign, and faithful to life in the stone as well as the flower. The feeling has spread among "Trevena's" few critical American admirers who have written about him, that he is fundamentally morbid and one-sided. On the contrary, we know of few novelists who are more recklessly and irresistibly gay, in whom sheer fun bubbles over so spontaneously and wholeheartedly. . . . His habit of confining a single novel to a single mood or passion of nature, together with the fact that Americans have only had an opportunity to read the novels which deal with her cruelest moods, have done the creative work of "John Trevena" grave injustice. And "Matrimony," simply his masterpiece of poetic grace, is still practically unknown to the American public, though it surpasses the most lyrical passages in [Meredith's]*The Ordeal of Richard Feverel.* When we become familiar with his rounded achievement and read it in leisure and silence we shall not hesitate to rank him as a novelist with his only living English peers, George Moore and Thomas Hardy. He is of the English novelists' most majestic lineage. (O[xenham] 97-99)

One of the *New York Times*'"outings" of Trevena gives the reader an unintendedly amusing report from his publisher, Mitchell Kennerley: "Some time ago attention was called to the rumor that 'John Trevena' was a pseudonym used to veil the identity of a man who, under his own name, was known as the author of books quite distinct in character and subject from the Dartmoor novels. There was such an inviting quality of mystery in this rumor that we started an inquiry through 'Trevena's' American publisher, who was not at first aware of his author's anonymity. Mr. Kennerley at once investigated the matter in England." Kennerley confirms Henham as Trevena's real name, lists the early novels, and then adds: "'Henham has recently married and hates people. He had some years ago to give up office work in London and go to a sanitarium for tuberculosis on Dartmoor, where he was cured but forbidden [for reasons of his lungs] to go to town again. He is very unpopular with the natives, as he caricatures them rather savagely in his books. He despises all his work previous to 'Furze the Cruel.'" The columnist concludes that Trevena's "splendid work in fiction, however, remains to us uninjured by Mr. Henham's misanthropy" ("Books and the War" BR104; "Topics of the Week" BR566). As to Kennerley's role as Trevena's American publisher, another journalist remarked on his firm's "fondness for books that show the dark side of the consciousness–books of occultism, they might be called. . . . If he and Emily Brontë had been contemporaries, 'Wuthering Heights' would have borne his imprint" ("In the Field of Literary Endeavor" 10).

The "misanthrope" published the last of his twenty-seven novels, *Typet's Treasure* in 1927; in 1928,he is living at the fishing village of Porthmellon, a fishing cove about a mile south of Mevagissey, Cornwall, on the English Channel; in the 1930s, he is living in a thatched cottage called "The Nook," Verwood, Dorset,with Rose who rejoined him. "In conversation with the villagers of Verwood, February 1961," Tanguy reports that "Trevena's favourite occupation was walking on the moors for several hours a day with his golden retriever" (10). In one of the two letters Myrtle Henry apparently received (2 November 1932 and 28 February 1933), Trevena writes in the latter: "I am an old man now and have lost creative power. I am not likely to be heard of again" (30). We do hear *from* him for a final time in 1943–1944 when he no longer publishes his address in *Who's Who*. In 1946, Martin writes*of* him:

> John Trevena still lives at the little village of Ferndown [a few miles south of Verwood], in Dorset. His health is poor and he has written nothing for publication for nearly twenty years. In a letter to the present writer some years ago, he said; "I am an old man now, somewhat rambling in thought and unsteady in gait; quite incapable of serious study or any sustained effort, as you may have judged from my long silence." . . . I visited him during the [Second World War], several years after he had written the somewhat pathetic words quoted above. . . . When I asked the rather old and weary, but by no means shambling or forgetful man, for assistance in respect of biographical material, he replied, sadly: "Supposing that no one took much interest in me, I recently destroyed all records of my former life, including three volumes of Press cuttings, diaries, photos–everything went into the bonfire, not even a letter was spared. So nothing is left but a fading memory." Thus the critical study of Trevena's work can still be written, but a close psychological analysis, a personal study derived from the intimate diaries, is not now possible. (89)

Myrtle Henry reports that "with the sadness of the person who feels that his sincerest and finest production is to be forgotten, and who must know that much of that work is good, John Trevena now realizes his mistake in having always shunned publicity. It has been neither indifference nor a cultivated aloofness that has made the writer avoid his public. Here is an author who has unfortunately differentiated between knowing his readers and publicity" (26).

The General Register Office entered his death as 3 April 1948, aged 77, domiciled for several years at "Royd" cottage, Pine Glen Avenue, Ferndown, Hampreston Road, Wimborne, Dorset. The primary cause of death was "cardiac failure" with secondary "chronic pulmonary tubercle" (i.e., the tuberculosis bacillus). According to a letter from the Bournemouth Crematorium, 14 April 1961, he was cremated in conformity with his handwritten last will and testament without "any religious ceremony."[6] Cremation clearly calls into question Searle's statement that Henham/Trevena was "laid to rest" in Ferndown (11), not to mention that Ferndown's community burial ground is at All Saints' Church in Hampreston. Rose Henham, widow of the deceased and living at the same address, was the legal informant. She herself died from stroke, as recorded by the General Register Office, on 18 February 1960, age 84, at a nursing home in Queens Park, Bournemouth West.

---

6. "I desire that my remains shall be disposed of as simply and economically as is possible. Having become a member of the Cremation Society, and paid its fee during my lifetime for the cremation of my body, no other expenses beyond the conveyance of my remains from the place of my death to the nearest Crematorium should be necessary, as I do not wish for any religious ceremony, but merely request that my ashes shall be cast to the winds, or scattered within the garden of the Crematorium where the incineration has been carried out.

"I appoint my wife, Rose Henham, to be my Executor, and to her I Give and Bequeath the whole of my property, both real and personal, of which I may be possessed at the time of my death.

"Ernest G. Henham." (Tanguy 129a, Facsimile 15)

CHAPTER 4

A PIXY IN PETTICOATS (1906)

Certain pivotal texts have consistently generated from one century to another a classic richness and diversity of interpretation. But only a fluctuating consensus upholds many other texts as "canonical" over against alternatives that might perfectly well *also* be appreciated as excellent, if not of Homeric or Shakespearian preeminence. John Trevena's *A Pixy in Petticoats,* issued anonymously by Alston Rivers in 1906, is a powerful work of the Edwardian era, a neo-mystical tragedy "of one that lov'd not wisely but too well" (Shakespeare). A reviewer of *Pixy* in the *Liverpool Courier* observed that the novel is "delightful almost to the last page. It is full of vivacity and 'joie de vivre.' The piquancy of the narrative is sustained with wonderful success. . . . The story is built up with quite exceptional skill. The writing is consistently brilliant"("Publisher's Notice," *Pixy* 1908). It's been said that the difference between the great and the pedestrian in art is "so subtle and elusive that it cannot be explained." This may be "perfectly phrased," as Algernon Moncrieff effused, "and quite as true as any observation in civilized life should be"; but as a literary critic I am by profession of a school that thrives on explanations. Should readers of this present study not yet have discovered*Pixy*, I shall unapologetically ruin its surprise ending by expanding upon the Liverpool reviewer's nearly unnoticed caveat "almost"; that is, somewhere just before the novel's end something happens to the story's delightfulness. What does "almost" imply–that *Pixy* becomes disappointing? unamusing? No, it means Burrough dies a sacrificial victim to his romantic illusions. Not only that single reviewer had voiced regret the story didn't have a fairy tale ending with the lovers living happily ever after. A different, predictably genteel, reviewer felt it had "a needlessly tragic finish"(Rev. of *Pixy*, *Lloyds* 16). Galbraith commented: "This author's tendency toward violence is rather curious, in view of the fact that he is, I understand, a person of very delicate health" (BR402).The difference between *Pixy* and pedestrian fiction is its counter-intuitive insight. Yet it is never the situation *per se* but the way in which Trevena's imaginative circumstances come together–just as *Furze*attained greatness by an abrupt happily-ever-after finish.

Among Trevena's outstanding novels, this one has proved to be his most popular. Very like Trevena himself, who was compelled for his health to leave the polluted air of the cities, his novel's protagonist, John Burrough, has been dwelling on Dartmoor in an isolated cabin much like Trevena's solitary hut, recovering his respiratory vigor while working somewhat perfunctorily on a study of the moor's neolithic ruins. There he encounters Beatrice Pentreath, who is the novel's "pixy," her surname suggesting Cornwall's misty Celtic past of myth and folklore. Many names in Cornwall that take a prefix from the local area begin with *Pen*, "head," "headland," "promontory" (or*Tre*, "farm," and*Pol*, "pond"). Pentreath means "end of the headland," almost as in Land's End (*Penn-an-wlas* in Cornish). In the antiquary Richard Carew's*Survey of Cornwall* (1811) we have the folk-rhyme: "By Tre, Pol, and Pen, /You shall know the Cornishmen" (149). It's been said that if names do not begin thus, they will probably begin with Saint because, as the common saying goes, "there are more saints in Cornwall than in Heaven." Since Beatrice's surname is*Pen*, she is not one of the Cornish saints; indeed, her incapacity for empathy goes to the heart of this narrative, which one may call a tragicomedy inasmuch as the grim denouement emerges from the comedy of the protagonist's passion. Trevena's underlying vision in this emotionally forceful tale bears on the entanglements of modern life which beget physical and spiritual sickness and bring about a tormenting sense that man neither can reach spiritual wholeness by his own reason nor control happiness by his own volition. But in contrast to Hardy's Doomsters, the diabolic in Trevena appears somehow balanced by an unseen power of beauty. Although there is "that inborn cruelty common to all living things in Nature" (*Pixy* 72), there is also a mystical primordial Ideal that, elusive though it may be, provides the spiritual buoyancy needed to live in the real world: "there must be a soul-world somewhere, for the mind has felt it"(*Granite* 288). In chapter seven, Trevena's indebtedness to Frederic Myers's seminal study *Human Personality* (1903) will be examined: "It may even be," similarly writes

Myers, "that some World-Soul is perennially conscious of all its past; and that individual souls, as they enter into deeper consciousness, enter into something which is at once reminiscence and actuality" (1:31).

The year following his 1910 marriage, Henham/Trevena was living with Rose in Sticklepath village, parish of South Tawton, continuing to write novels located in this Dartmoor area (1911 census). Trevena's ethnographic technique of recording social observations was a rooted aspect of his style. The young Henham said of *Menotah* (1897): "The local colour is simply so much word photography" and the "characters in this work are for the most part actual life studies" (Prefatory Note). Not only can the same be said of his most expensively produced volume, the memoir-like *Adventures* with its mountain characters and its life studies of plants, but as has been pointed out the identity of thefiguresin most of his novels was so close to reality that they recognized themselves and their neighbors in his texts. Perhaps not coincidentally Beatrice-the-Pixy's name is true to life–a Beatrice Pentreath was born in 1880 at Plymouth, Devonshire, and until her September 1904 marriage lived in Penzance, Cornwall, which was the fictional Beatrice's adjacent home locality as well. However, this original Beatrice was of a working class background (her father was a carpenter, so she probably didn't sport "a jewelled butterfly" hatpin, symbolic though it may be of her personality) and she was born 15 January 1880, not on leap year day 1880 as in the novel: "I celebrated my fifth birthday two years ago. . . . I was born, you see, on the twenty-ninth of February" (102). But the actual Beatrice's age when the novel was published still tallied exactly with the fictional Beatrice's age since 1900 was *not* a leap year. Also the age of the smitten Burrough matched that of Henham/Trevena, still thirty-five in the summer of 1906. Although by 1906 the historical Beatrice had been married, Trevena might have met such a charmer on Dartmoor possibly during the summer of 1903 or 1904, perhaps there also for its "open-air treatment." In the novel, old Miss Pentreath "had seen various young people, to say nothing of those somewhat past that state, engaged in what she regarded as the very laudable practice of love-making. They may have been mere summer flirtations, but at a distance it looked like the real thing" (187). If the real Beatrice had been engaged to her

Penzance accountant in 1903 or 1904 but was indulging in a "mere summer flirtation" with Henham, then the imaginary Beatrice's avoidance of even the appearance of intimacy with Burrough has a very practical origin. She returns in *The Dartmoor House that Jack Built* for somewhat more than a cameo appearance, characteristically retelling legends, and afterwards just disappears over the moors. Even more intriguing, when in 1910 Henham/Trevena married Selina Rose McDonald, his bride gave her age as thirty on the marriage license although according to census records she had been born in Canada ten years earlier in 1870. Could she have been pretending to be still within the authentic Beatrice Pentreath's child-bearing years, to be that girl who genuinely *was* the age Rose only claimed to be? On the 1911 census record, the new bride Selina Rose Henham gave her age as 31 and her birthplace as "London Holloway, London"; but according to the General Register Office no such person (*née* McDonald) was born there during the years 1879–1881.

A Pixy in Petticoats as a title would be for any serious novel of "to-day" as outdated as that hyphenated Edwardian spelling–short of satire, perhaps. Further, "pixy" *alliterating* with "petticoats" contains its own strategic chronological contrast–the by-then discredited Devonshire fairies of olden times conjoined with the then-fashionable petticoats of serpentine flounces in moirée or taffeta. But it may help also to realize that Trevena's petticoated pixy was undoubtedly an incarnation sanctioned by Samuel Taylor Coleridge's sixteen-line ode on the fairies of Devonshire, "Songs of the Pixies," first published in 1796. This poem has been described as Coleridge's "first attempt to re-invent a poetic world of natural emblems, in which the imagination stealthily transforms the everyday into the visionary" (Holmes 51). During the summer holiday of 1793, Coleridge had stayed with family in Ottery St. Mary in Devonshire. In a prose Preface to his poem, Coleridge gives the scene and history of the poem's genesis:

> The Pixies, in the superstition of Devonshire, are a race of beings invisibly small, and harmless or friendly to man. At a small distance from a village in that county, half-way up a wood-covered hill, is an excavation called the Pixies' Parlour. The roots of old trees form its ceiling; and on its sides are innumerable cyphers, among which the author discovered his

> own cypher and those of his brothers, cut by the hand of their childhood. At the foot of the hill flows the river Otter.
>
> To this place the Author, during the summer months of the year 1793, conducted a party of young ladies; one of whom, of stature elegantly small, and of complexion colourless yet clear, was proclaimed the Faery Queen. On which occasion the following Irregular Ode was written.

Perhaps with Coleridge in mind, Trevena writes: "Burrough was a scholar, and therefore a fool in love. . . . How many would confess to the initials they had carved on beech-trees? . . . To the doggerel they had penned, or the mad phrases they had mouthed? Every wise man is a Bedlamite [lunatic] for a few hours of his life" (34). Coleridge seems to have been attracted to a number of petticoats at this time; notwithstanding, critics have identified the fairy Queen as a Miss Beautflour to whom his amatory effusion was addressed. Running throughout it are echoes of Shakespeare's Queen Mab in *A Midsummer Night's Dream* and John Milton's *Allegro* and *Il Penseroso* as well as *Comus*. Also, inasmuch as Coleridge quoted the phrase "unknown to fame" from Alexander Pope's translation of the *Iliad* (2.394), perhaps one may also find something of Pope's sylphs in the pixies' confession of eavesdropping on rustic love-talk and tampering with its outcome. Implicit in the whole thrust of "Songs" is the antithesis between a supernatural, timeless beauty and a mortal sorrow or passion (a contrast already integral to Trevena's vision and similar to that which later found its way into W.B. Yeats's "The Stolen Child"). At least three further scenic and characterological elements from Coleridge's "Songs" are carried directly into *Pixy*: the "elegantly small" girl as Queen of the fairies; the enamored presence of Coleridge "unknown to fame" echoed by the novel's anonymous author and by Burrough; and the "Parlour" that becomes in Trevena's novel a "secret nook," Blissland. But Coleridge's parlor at Ottery should not be confused with another "Pixies' Parlour" described in Eden Phillpotts's*Children of the Mist*, a fantastic pile of five giant rocks on Dartmoor that "form a sort of rude chamber, sacred to fairy folk since a time before the memory of the living" (2-3).

As to the more deeply-drawn personages in *Pixy*, John Burrough, as the author's persona, seems closer to mainstream expressions of the intellective "sensations and ideas" drawn from a range of nineteenth-century aesthetic heroes. In Trevena's most extreme presentations of mood and mind, creations are tinged with the anagogic, the enigmatic, and the paranormal. In *Pixy,* Beatrice Pentreath's personality surely fits in here; she emerges as the spirit of Dartmoor's earth and sky, less a social butterfly than Pope's sylphs but undoubtedly more a pixy than Miss Beautflour. Under the tutelage in childhood of an aged "black witch," Beatrice (a descendant of the witchy and historical Dolly Pentreath) becomes the petticoat form of the winds, heather, granite, furze and fern of Dartmoor, "which exaggerates everything; adding fierceness to fierceness, colour to colour, strength to strength" (*Furze* 64). She is like a Greek Nereid or nymph–a beautiful maiden who in dance and song animates the specific locale to which she is inseparably bound as its playful *genius loci*. She is "not lovely, not even pretty, as beauty goes," but despite her lack of conventional beauty an intense sexuality is woven through every nuance of her life's fabric: "Beauty appeals to the eye. Beatrice appealed to the five senses" (*Pixy* 62).

Pixies, says one of Trevena's sources, cited earlier, were probably "contemporaneous" with the gods of antiquity; but if not, then "we must seek among the gnomes and pixies for the descendants of the dryads and nymphs who once presided over the woods and fountains" ("Pleasant Land of Devon" 431). Nymphs were associated with mountains and life-giving springs that watered the river-gods:

> Living in the mountains, nymphs . . . rank neither with mortals nor with immortals: a long time do they live, eating heavenly food and treading a lovely dance among the immortals; and with them the Sileni and the sharp-eyed Slayer of Argus mate in the depths of pleasant caves. . . . When they are born, firs and oaks with lofty boughs spring out of the earth that nurtures men, beautiful, flourishing trees on the high mountains. And men call them sacred places of the immortals, and no mortal lops them with an ax. But when the fate of death is near at hand for them, first those lovely trees become dry and their bark shrivels away, then the branches drop off; and at the same time the life of the nymph goes out as it leaves the light of the sun. (*Homeric Hymn to Aphrodite* 257-261; 264-272)

Lone travelers sometimes secretly observed these elemental creatures bathing nude–as several townsfolk did of Beatrice. But in modern life, in contrast to antiquity, this unity of consciousness and nature "could no longer be solved, as in Phryne ascending naked out of the water, by perfection of bodily form, or any joyful union with the external world: the shadows had grown too long, the light too solemn, for that" (Pater, *Renaissance* 228).

In the opening chapter, Burrough's discovery of Beatrice's Friday-like footprint and a crumpled newspaper are oddly juxtaposed with his project of writing a book on the moor's pre-historic remains. The "Pleasant Land of Devon," drawn on by Trevena, had remarked: "If anything were needed to enhance the solemnity with which Nature has invested the weird waste of Dartmoor, it would be found in the footprints left by the races which once inhabited it" (425-426). Both "footprints" are clues indicative of human presences, but one is the print of a living person and the other belongs to an ancient past. Although Defoe's Crusoe had admitted that he missed companionship, his equally unhappy speculations following upon his discovery of the footprint suggest he may be conflicted about human contact. The newspaper with its red stains also prompts for Burrough images of "sickness, sorrowing, suffering, and death" (*Pixy* 7). If Crusoe is hesitant to return to society, might not Burrough also unconsciously prefer isolation, and might not it have been better if his isolation had continued? However, even before he has seen Beatrice in the flesh his imagination is instantly obsessed with the phantom pixy's mark. Here also begins Trevena's authorial self-ridicule at being "pixy-led" to such a degree. Later in her presence Burrough is unable to take his eyes off her face, skin, undergarments, and body language: "Her hair, which had long ago discarded all pins and fastenings, streamed about her, and she had twisted the ends about her waist, and walked holding it. The wind stretched her scanty clothing tightly upon her and revealed every line from waist to ankle. She looked the very spirit of health and strength. She suggested the pixy queen or the white witch of Cranmere" (147). And her periodic absences only enhance the distraction that disrupts his archeological project.

Beguilingly saucy, fresh, and unconventional as an elemental spirit, Beatrice also exhibits a selfish and heartless side, a pride both in her physical fitness that renders her unable to accept Burrough's accidental disfigurement and in her all-too-strong sense of family, social rank, and economic status proclaimed by her "lace-trimmed petticoat" (28). She values her untrammeled independence among Dartmoor's springs and clefts and is ambivalent about loving an impoverished writer such as Burrough. She asks that he call her "Bill" and adopts an infantilized femininity–"you'm a mucky twoad" (101)–to encourage yet control his naive adoration. Because she is so drawn to the intense impressions of each outward moment and so engrossed by "romance and legend" and the dreams of her "wild Cymric imagination" (183,125), Beatrice does not like having serious discussions about the future. Her playful façade is partly Peter Pan's refusal to grow up–J.M. Barrie's play had debuted to immediate popular success on 27 December 1904–and (if this *is* different) partly also a specific avoidance of Burrough's romantic advances owing to a fear of emotional entrapment. Her conflicted sense of love harks back to a troubled family history, a sportsman father whose clerical duties were handled by a curate and a deceased mother, leaving her to live with an elderly aunt, her shadow double. This elder Miss Pentreath has spent much of her life with emotional rejection, obsessively painting her face to stem the encroachments of age, dressing with a pathetically youthful inappropriateness, and seeking to marry almost any male of her social class. Finally, when escorted by "an elderly and short-sighted clergyman" to a traveling menagerie, she is deconstructed by a troop of apes:

> There was a cageful of monkeys, and the coquettish lady stood before it, and poked playfully at the progenitors of her species with a beribboned parasol. Suddenly an ape seized the ferrule, and drew her close to the cage. Instantly a dozen paws shot forth, hat and hair vanished, while a general disrobing process went on below. The short-sighted clergyman became very properly aghast at the appearance of the lay-figure, which continued to undergo the throes of transformation–a sort of rough rehearsal of what he might expect the night after "The voice that breathed o'er Eden" had been sung for his benefit. (75)

As Beatrice confronts her own desire and fear of entrapment, she recalls instances of sinners locked into a limbo of pain: Tregeagle with his Sisyphus-like tasks or the ghost of a wicked clergyman plugged for the last century in "an empty bottle of Hollands" (186). Beatrice banteringly threatens to release this predecessor of the current vicar, the senile old Yeoland in whom desire has outlived performance, when he entices her to sit in his arm-chair, a sort of compact love-nest or *baisodrome*.

In the mythic fantasies of nineteenth-century Romantic Platonism, the fusion of Platonic and medieval Christian ideals of love becomes Trevena's counter-vision to the rationalism of the Enlightenment and militant humanism. Plato's *Phaedrus* and *Symposium* had described an infinite and supreme Beauty as the archetype or template for the highest love within the phenomenal world. Burrough, as a scholar-writer-dreamer, believes he has caught a glimpse of Ideal Beauty but his sad acquiescence in Beatrice's horror at his disfigurement, rooted in her Pixyish pagan materialism, lands him instead in a purgatorial anomie. Like "La Belle Dame sans Merci" in John Keats's ballad, Beatrice is the *femme fatale* who incites men to pursue their dreams of Beauty's elusive self but who, within her world limited to physical reality, can nevercome to be an authentic symbol of transfigured nature. In an effort to catch sight of Beatrice after she has returned to Cornwall, Burrough travels to Land's End where Lethowsow or the lost Kingdom of Lyonesse, said to border Cornwall, had sunk beneath the sea. This lost land with its Holy Grail epitomizes the spiritual wholeness or elusive transcendental realm that Trevena had called "a soul-world." Into Burrough's musings Trevena interpolates Sir Thomas Mallory's scene of Launcelot entering the Castle of Corbenic to glimpse, only briefly, the Grail (Mallory 3:169-170). In the modern world, this Golden Age is past and will not come again; the Pixies are extinct and the Kingdom of Lyonesse lost under the waves. Nevertheless, Trevena refuses to accept the corpse of belief as irreducible and ultimate. Those ruled by the heart still can experience the transformative power of the Grail, not as a literally existent reality–that would be to make of it a monumental illusion–but as a power within love that nurtures contact with an inconceivable Divine Presence.

A French onion-seller wandering across the moors, very much an iconic figure like Wordsworth's leech-gatherer, knocks on Burrough's cottage door. But unlike Wordsworth's apparition who testifies to an innate power in mind and nature, Trevena's visitor expresses a personal gratitude for the sheltering presences of "Our Lady and the blessed saints"who have sustained his family (277). Similarly when the angelic Paolina, who took her own life yet was so radically pure she went directly to Heaven, leaned over a precarious railing she felt no danger "because 'The saints and angels take care of us, signore'" (*Adventures* 157, 161-162). Burrough cannot square such relics of literal belief with the hard facts of contemporary life–for him that age of unquestioning faith has gone. And yet, has he not allowed the illusion of Beatrice as a living pixy to tyrannize him? Not long afterwards, among the rains and ruins of the season's encroaching winter, another Frenchman lies drowned in Beatrice's medieval church, an unavoidable parallel to Burrough's encounter. With a saddened sense of her own mortality, Beatrice recites the words of "the pre-reformation order of matrimony" (*Pixy* 294), groping for some drawing together of past and present, one faith dead, "the other powerless to be born" (Arnold). But her ensuing rationale for accepting Burrough's proposal of marriage is delimited by the material and the non-symbolic. She allows the chance winds and leaves of nature to confirm the issue for her, the seasonal primrose to appoint the time of the marriage, and the pixies at the Cranmere letterbox to disclose to Burrough her decision–all without any inkling of love as an avenue to a higher spiritual reality.

Trevena's deeply felt spiritual sensibility looked to new possibilities in ancient liturgy and doctrine, as his story "Matrimony" suggests. Composed only six months before his own marriage, this spiritualistic account, which also cites Beatrice's excerpt from the marriage service of the medieval church, evinces how for true lovers "all matter became absorbed in symbolism" by their mutual devotion (330). The transcendental symbol, throwing together what the diabolic has fractured, recreates the "dead time's exploded dream" (Arnold again) in the form of a deepened interpretation and transformation of the physical. In "Matrimony" Trevena implies that the lovers' vision of nature–which remains viable for modern man–is sacramentally tantamount to their ancient and literal miracle of marriage:

> Behind them the sun, in front a bush of holly on fire with berries and sunset; nothing more. One bush of holly among hundreds, and yet something was there they had never seen before; a glory, a transfiguration; the bush burnt and was not consumed. During those few moments every sense was satisfied, nothing more was needed, no other ceremony, no more Sacramental presence, not even a kiss. Life had risen high, run over, and the part that was spilled passed down and melted into the light on that holly-bush. And then, though the sun had not gone, the colour was there no longer; the bush became cold and as the others, the fire went out; and as Anthonie and Petronel watched the sacred embers dying, and the berries darkening one by one, they clung to each other again, frightened no longer, but full of happiness and hope. (319)

Because God himself spoke to Moses out of the celestial fire, nature's "transfiguration" is here symbolic of His potency within the beauty of material objects. Although the self may be assailed and life's balance traduced by the randomness of circumstance, the mind captures a higher reality than is present on earth in anypurely natural state. Without the symbol's sacramental rebonding of the fallen and broken, "earth would be joined to heaven, no more with sunbeams, but by a web of hopeless dreams" (341). Here the quest for a return to Eden is sanctioned by symbolic vision, enabling the self to see the external world anew as no longer disenchanted but as the *symbolon* of a Beauty in which its greatest happiness consists. One imagines Beatrice's observation that "the idea of husband and wife being one is very pretty, and equally impossible while human nature remains as it is" (*Pixy* 184) may not be up to Trevena's standards.

Cranmere pool, source of all rivers, is celebrated as the Pixies' magical site of love; yet here tragedy overlays the quest for an ideal love. Trevena observes that if classical nymphs personify the outflow of springs into the rivers as gods, then the Dart is "not so much a river bringing water to the people as a god who demands tribute from them. That tribute was "a human heart each year–one year the heart of a maid, the next that of a man, and so on for ever"(125). Trevena adds, "One cannot wonder if the Celtic moormen should have peopled this desolate region of crevice and tarn with the souls of sinners. Here was once the site of purgatory" (127), a trope suggested by "The Pleasant Land of Devon" (424).

Trevena quotes from *The Elder Eddas* to foreshadow Burrough's ultimate fate. This quotation, in slightly augmented form reads: "I saw the day's star, the sun, sink to its roaring home; andbehind me I heard Hell's latticed doors creaking ponderously shut. . . . Since that gloomy day I never saw the sun again, for the mountain waters closed over me" (Sigfusson 39-45). The next morning the supernatural world of the Cornish sinner Tregeagle, whose story Beatrice had just retold, is put into contrast with Burrough's practical world of hurt. Bracketed on either side by exploding artillery shells, one might think Burrough resembles Tregeagle caught between damnation and salvation. But Tregeagle, whose life is darkened at its source by the diabolic, at least exists in a moral universe–the army's technical missteps have no moral import at all.

If one were to assume *Pixy* was based on some actual moorland affair, then its brilliance is the way in which Trevena has turned that interlude into a deeper allegory of love's symbolic possibilities. The most eerie image in the narrative is Beatrice's dream of having "done something wicked or foolish" and finding a nameless "thing" growing ever-larger among the furze-reek in the moonlight under her window, "the consequence of what I had done" (*Pixy* 202). As an uncanny figure of illicit love and the shame of an ensuing pregnancy following her "night of enchantment" (318), this would rank among the most Freudian of dreams in the Edwardian era. Pondering Burrough's marriage proposal, Beatrice recalls an incident found in the "Diurnal" of an Anglican country parson who in 1665 laid the ghost of a young woman, Dorothy Dinglet, who was "unquiet" in her grave "because of a certain sin" (Hawker 173). Owing to his polite readership, Trevena allowed his fictional Beatrice to offer a more-genteel but misleading interpretation of the dream: her growing repugnance for Burrough's disfigurement. Yet Beatrice and Burrough's overnight in Tom-tit-tot's palace might well have culminated in a moment of passion, and her repudiation of him may well be a projectionof her own alarming fears of an aftermath. That her hasty morning departure was either the consequence of having done "something wicked or foolish" or a desperate effort to avoid such an act, seems much the stronger but unusable interpretation.

Just before Beatrice returns to Cornwall, Burrough's cat Peter "had gone out upon the moor and had never come back," shot by the sadistic Willum(*Pixy* 322). Burrough always spoke to Peter as if he magically understood, like an attendant spirit in animal form. And his love of Beatrice also mythologized her as if she were pixy or nymph. If Peter and Beatrice embody an enchantment that vanishes like an illusion, their loss may forecast Burrough's own disappearance. Like his cat, Burrough too will go out on the moor and never come back. One would like to imagine that the "pixy-led" (90) Burrough is devoured by the Dart as a sacrifice to the life of sun and moon, the rain and the mountains. But in the new era of rationality his death is merely the pursuit of an illusion, flawed judgment. Yet one might note that when Burrough, the alter ego of Henham/Trevena, disappears in the sleet, cold, and mist of Cranmere, the author is not merely self-referencing the winter rigors of his former Canadian pursuits; rather, his protagonist's fate becomes an analogue for the author's own outworn identity–Henham will vanish and "never come back" so that after this anonymous novel the author may return as Trevena. To what *Pixy* does this rebirth belong?

CHAPTER 5

"OLD BAILEY'S WOOING" (1906)
ARMINEL OF THE WEST (1907)

"Old Bailey's Wooing"

In the same year that *Pixy* (1906) appeared, Ernest Henham published his first short Dartmoor story, "Old Bailey's Wooing," under his own name in one of Britain's leading literary periodicals, *Macmillan's Magazine* (retitled for his 1910 story collection "Froggie Would a-Wooing Go!"). It is a transition piece to what might dramatically be called–with apologies to scholars of heroic folklore–the "Matter of Dartmoor." Not that the breadth and complexity of versions and variants in Trevena's new subject are equal to the "Matter of Troy" or the "Matter of Arthur"; but we are presented in his narratives of Dartmoor with unfolding or overlapping ranges of interpretation, very much as in those antique "matters" or subjects of folklore. Among the most successful novels set on Dartmoor had been Arthur Conan Doyle's *The Hound of the Baskervilles* (1902), which owed its melancholy Gothic countryside as much to Edgar Allan Poe's "The Fall of the House of Usher" as to Dartmoor itself.On account of Doyle's success, fiction "about Devon in the twentieth century has been dominated by the idea of 'landscape' for its own sake, which has tended to undermine the human interest" (Beeson 162). Although Eden Phillpotts may depend upon emotions stimulated by landscape settings to the neglect of character development or significantly evolving images and meanings, the same cannot be said of Hardy or Trevena. Indeed, "Old Bailey's Wooing" is all about the revelation of character. It is a comic pen-portrait, like many of those in *Furze* and elsewhere, with blistering satire on the avarice of apparently Christian men and women, a tale written with suppressed contempt for the wealthy Old Bailey's greedy scheming to get his hands on the widow Sal's money. In the light of Trevena's story, "Matrimony," one may well imagine what the author thought of Bailey's motivations for undertaking his third marriage.

Henham/Trevena's story clearly has elements to which he turns again both in *Arminel* (the "theft" of land from the Duchy of Cornwall or the farmer courting the wealthy, obese Sal) and then in *Furze* (Tavistock Goose Fair). Could this story as the first of his Matter of Dartmoor be a "feeler" as to how well his treatment of this new local color subject might be accepted by high-profile publishers? At any rate, fictionally "Old Bailey's Wooing" aligns itself less with the magical folklore and poetic prose of *Pixy* than with the satiric social realism of *Furze*. Henham tells his story seemingly in a style of objective representation, with an unflagging attention to the naturalistic, material world of local time and space, to concrete motivation, and to physical peculiarities. His social observations, depicted with sheer exuberance, are not an uncontrolled transcript from a directly-observed reality but disclose a deliberate, ironic slant or selectiveness of observation, a realism stranger than fiction. Yet although the author eschews the more intangible reaches of reflection and emotion, his characters' inner thoughts are largely implied or revealed by juxtapositions of apparently casual images or unforced details. Thus objectivity is not sacrificed to moralistic or edifying commentary; and the indictment of pride and greed emerges through an artfully dramatic simplicity and in dry ironic understatement. His descriptions–such as the lovers walking close together because "the lane was very narrow and the widow was not" (*Written . . . Rain* 268) or Bailey's proposal coming out in scripted bursts of inarticulate wooing lost among greedy silences–carries a condemnation of rustic practice and principles even beyond the censoriousvoices of high seriousness.

The basic plot conflict is conveyed by Bailey's mock-epic dreams of the dancing gold sovereigns–Sal's £80 per annum income–and Sal's daughter's dreams of opening a lady's academy in Plymouth. As Bailey crosses wits with the fat lady, his looming fate becomes subliminally anticipated by the reader; but it is only in the final ironic plot twist when Sal assigns her complete portfolio to her daughter's project that the reader fully recognizes that Sal's total truth-telling about her financial intentions creates, as she intends, the perfect trap for the overly-confident Bailey. He misjudges her motivations and assumes she is lying because his greed doesn't reckon on intangible priorities when it comes to her child. Sal's daughter matters emotionally to her more than Bailey's family does to him; therefore, when Bailey, according to his script, weds on Goose Fair Day, the reader begins to see he is well acquainted already with one goose. The story's last words say it all: instead of paying *his* bills with *her* money, Bailey had to "submit to a sermon from his wife upon the sin of covetousness, which was no doubt good for him; but those who ought to know say that old Bailey has aged considerably since his marriage" ("Old Bailey" 918). In the 1910 revision, Trevena ends: ". . . old Bailey has become very peevish since the third and last time he went a-wooing" (*Written . . . Rain*277). Given Sal's craftiness, a "sermon" coming from her is certainly hypocritical; but Bailey's aging at his loss of the widow's income is morally worse since the works and days of one's life ought to be of much greater value than a superfluity of golden sovereigns. Unlike Chaucer's implicit respect for the figure of Christ hidden under the features of his pilgrims, Henham/Trevena here lifts the mask of social propriety to expose, much like his immediate predecessor Guy deMaupassant, nothing at all beneath the greed–only punishment with a fearful aptness.

Arminel of the West

Arminel of the West (1907) is the first novel to carry Henham's new pen-name, "John Trevena." The title's "West" is what oncehad been the West Saxon kingdoms which at the transition from the nineteenth to the twentieth century was England's impoverished southwest region. Arminel is the daughter of Jack Zaple, "Dartmoor Jack," who as a clever young man insinuated his way into the ranks of the commoners by gradually expanding his occupancy of the moorland without any title or right. In this same spirit, his daughter Arminel acquires the education and manners of gentry and with deliberate purpose gains acceptance by the closed society of "old" West Country families. Her given name is the feminine form of Herman, the original meaning of which was "army" combined with "man." Arminel is thus, perhaps, a female warrior no longer fighting a physical enemy with sword and buckler; rather, she has pitted herself against the socially constructed values of a narrowly patriarchal and decaying class system. Arminel contrasts herself to the simpering heroine of "early Victorian and penny novelette style" (258) though she is not quite a proto-modern, fin-de-siècle phenomenon of the New Woman. This was a period of transition and active campaigning for women's suffrage; women had emerged out of the Victorian feminist rebellion but continued to be denied rights. Since specific roles and objectives of the feminist movement were inconsistently defined by supporters and opponents, all one can say is that feminism was felt to be an agent of social change, good or bad. As to a women's new outlets in the workplace and her increasing sexual freedom, Trevena's view of her role is middle of the road.

Whereas his stereotypical Victorian woman only "simpers," Arminel is defined by an upward social mobility: she has an education combined with the conventional female employment as a teacher. Yet, more importantly, she is dismissed for exceeding genteel middle-class standards. Also, Arminel is absorbed into the class system by being stronger than the males; however, she falls back on traditional feminine wiles, including pregnancy, to solidify her place. As to the other women in this novel, the obese are anything but "male identified"; they too wear the pants in their social world, although Arminel wears hers more stylishly, like slim-ankle contour slacks. At root this is a sort of modern gender equality since the female has appropriated the traditional privileges of patriarchal male supremacy for the sake of keeping social order. Yet for Nona Wistman in this tale, sexual freedom spells disaster; there can be no gender equality for pregnancy out of wedlock. It may not be amiss to suggest Trevena was aware of the difficulty of reconciling the changing social role of marriage with its sacramental history. In Thomas Hardy's *Jude the Obscure* (1896), for example, Sue Bridehead is a victim of the double standard of morality owing to the hypocrisies of Victorian marriage; but Trevena, unlike Hardy, does not wish to sacrifice the sacredness of marriage because it conflicts with natural human impulse. Rather, Arminel renegotiates relations between the sexes by reconciling the time-honored institution of marriage with feminine equality.

Reviewers had found Beatrice in *Pixy* fast, flippant, and vulgar whereas they felt Arminel was "charming," seemingly evaluating the heroines in both these narratives as if they themselves were personally required to love them. One even objected with full Victorian prudery to the author's "drawing lurid, sensational pictures," "dwelling only on the grosser side of passion," "ever on the alert to catch a gleam of prurience," and "in comparison . . . 'Jude the Obscure' is innocuous"–all of this added up to a presumably young writer with a "curious lack of reticence" (Rev. of *Pixy*, *Academy* 393). Writing of *Pixy* and *Arminel*, Lewis Melville observed: "Contrasting the two books, one feels that in the first the characters ran away with their creator; in the second there is no question but that he has his team well in hand. . . . In 'A Pixy in Petticoats,' apart from the two principal actors, one remembers only Beatrice's aunt; . . . but in 'Arminel of the West' it is easy to conjure up several well-drawn characters who are germain to the story." Melville cites the two Challacombes, the hero's aunt and father, and the Wistmans–father, mother, and Nona the daughter (BR157). He might have added, at the very least, several servants, the village idiot, and a dog. Cooper echoes Melville's comparison: "'A Pixy in Petticoats' is easily the most haphazard of his volumes, the one that shifts its key most unexpectedly, the one that depends most largely upon the element of chance." Although *Pixy*, he says, failed to solve the "painful psychological problem" of disfigurement and love, *Arminel* poses "more serious and widespread problems," unfortunately however still with "a certain inconclusiveness." For Cooper this internally ambiguous or unstable storyline in these two novels has only been transcended in the "epic sweep" of the trilogy that follows, with its underlying "wise and easily comprehended symbolism." We notice, however, that he begins to find this admirable "sweep" too much of a good thing when he hints at problems with "tangled" plot threads (335, 330, 333).

That a novel should avoid spontaneity or the provisional–either as a conscious strategy or an intuitive outcome–is currently regarded as an outdated touchstone. That the novelist should prefer "sweep" to the contrasting technique of psychological focus–as in the interactions of an all-but-isolated young couple on the moor–is, again, an imposed, not an authentic aesthetic value. And, of course, solving the dilemma of disfigurement and love is not Trevena's self-appointed task–in one of his strongest short stories, "A Human

Bundle" in *Temple Bar* (1897), the whole pathos of the mutilation is concentrated in the last scene by the reader *not*knowing the outcome, only dreading what it probably will be. The reviewers are correct in identifying an increasing number of characters; but from *Pixy* through the trilogy or quartet of novels concluding with *Bracken* (1910)–and beyond–Trevena's technique and vision may more profitably be seen as anticipating the new emphasis on mental and emotional aspects in psychological realism. Moreover, when these reviewers call *Pixy* and *Arminel* "fairy stories," they are putting Trevena's new wine into childhood's old wine-skins. Often he will allow several disparate threads of satire, intertextuality, or appropriation-with-a-twist to disrupt linear narration.But these threads eventually intertwine, to make a collective or aggregate ensemble, perhaps even a metaphysical or elementally "grand narrative." Trevena combines the richness of local-color folklore and reality with an outcome of unexpected intensity. While not denying the existence of sorrow and failure, he never accepts an all-inclusive, unequivocal defeat for the human spirit. Whether in any particular plot he withholds or allows fulfillment of the heart's desires, inherent in his storytelling is always the possibility for some sudden alteration and disclosure of a marvelous, underlying power overturning tragedy.

Arminel opens with Giglet Fair on the first Saturday of December–an unpropitious chilly season for the romantic premise that young men and women may address each other without introductions. But it serves for the beginning of a romance between the upper class Brian Challacombe, recently arrived for the benefit of his lungs at the Dartmoor home of his status-conscious aunt, and Arminel, the oilman's daughter, returned to her home after being dismissed from her first teaching position. Arminel's lady-like airs and her socially avant-garde, educated, independent spirit raise the issue of her social respectability when she becomes more the pursuer of Brian than the pursued as she slyly pinches the distracted young man. Never in serious competition with Arminel for Brian's honorable intentions is pretty Nona Wistman, daughter of the local eccentric Anglican rector (who may be, again, among Trevena's most grotesquely caricatured versions of his own adoptive uncle). Nona has been artificially kept from learning about the world and her own sexuality by being penned up in a room with only her Bible, church school materials, and mathematical practice problems. Wistman's narrow and bitterly conservative morality, together with the curse of poverty, has destroyed both his wife and daughter: "He is a half-mad fanatic, who has driven his weak, poor-spirited wife to the verge of lunacy, and having brooded upon the world, the flesh, and the devil in his unintelligent way, strains every nerve to keep his daughter in ignorance of those things that are natural to human creatures. In his efforts to made her believe love is for God only, and not for man, he never lets her speak to any one of the opposite sex, nor read a story, nor even have girl friends; so that at the age of twenty 'she was entirely innocent'" (Melville BR157).

When Brian speaks to Nona, she is so flustered by this singular encounter that she cannot respond graciously: "The girl's distress was painful. She was more than frightened; horrified at being addressed by a man, alone, in the porch, with her father's deep voice in her ears. She became perfectly white and drew back with a shiver" (61). The trouble with cultivating such unworldliness out of ignorance is that biblical stories and poetry such as the Song of Solomon do not appear entirely allegorical to Nona as she ultimately enters puberty. With her naive chastity rotting at the core, she circumvents her father's imprisonment and throws herself at Brian. He, like his father and generations of male Challacombes previously, cannot resist sexual opportunity. Wistman's suppression of his daughter's natural drives thus emerges in a wholly destructive way; and when the vicar can no longer manage her rebellion, she is sent off to an Anglican nunnery so regressive in its discipline and rites that it is more medieval than any convent, even ludicrously pre-Christian pagan in its religious observations. But when the nuns discover Nona is pregnant, she is sent back to the rectory and Wistman pursues Brian to force a marriage.

Brian truly wants to marry Arminel, not Nona. Trevena is clear about the physicality of Brian's desires for Arminel when he proposes to her. Though bowdlerized into a bump on her forehead, he kisses her "mount of Venus" (Latin *mons veneris*); she says he is the ogre who wants to "take me to your castle and eat me"; and then he looks "and saw that her eyes were open" (167, 169). But after having secretly married her, the temperamentally weak Brian is afraid to confess to Arminel that Nona had seduced him, and he vacillates about introducing her as his new wife to his father and his aunt. Although Nona and Arminel were both pursuers of Brian, their reasons and characters are widely different; Nona becomes hard and selfish whereas Arminel remains appealing and almost euphoric until misunderstandings bring the near certainty of tragedy. One theme in Trevena that essentially goes back as far as the guilty romance in *Tenebrae* (1898) is that of a dissembling, hypocritical passion rather than a free-spoken and joyfully hallowed love. Because *Arminel* is about breaking down limits on heart and imagination, a related theme becomes the evils of priestly celibacy, to which Trevena will return in *Sleeping Waters* (1913). Brian's father Cuthbert, an ex-priest from both the churches of Rome and England, has departed the virtuous and spiritual life of celibacy and chastity. His weakness for pretty girls is a function of his modern loss of that close, divine union of man and woman. Brian and Cuthbert always remain gentlemen, but the double standard was as present for them as it was for the earlier Victorians; and one sees why Trevena considered that for woman of culture and would-be standing, relationships defying traditional norms even in the era of the New Woman created complications.

Tragi-comic issues of power and control surface in Miss Challacombe's tyrannizing of Brian in the same manner thatshe bosses her servant Coneybear.Then in romance Brian is steered by both Arminel and Nona; and Nona in turn is dominated by her father, the Reverend Mr. Wistman. Trevena especially juxtaposes upper class sexual pursuits with lower class lovemaking; comic for the lower classes but potentially tragic for the upper. One can excuse Trevena's tendency to present the lower classes as having simpler relationships inasmuch as historically in comedy rustics could be counted upon to provide the author with humorous subplots to play off againstthe unfolding complications among more-sophisticated lovers. Coneybearpursues a corpulent owner of a bar for her money while simultaneously enjoying sex with the Wistman's maid–at least until her pregnancy when she gains the upper hand. And concurrently the elderly farmer Jonadab is also wooing the same barkeep as Coneybear while pursuing her equally obese sister as a backup. These barbed portraits of shammed emotions, greed, and drunkenness were much appreciated by readers. One reviewer singled out as classic farce both Jonadab's courtship and

Miss Challacombe's ludicrously comic reversal of roles, as she falls under the domination of her long-time servant Betsy, whose narrow but practical views run up against the aristocratic lady's eccentricities: "Her every encounter with the cook, who refuses to be discharged, is a delight. The mock Homeric descriptions of the courtship of two fat peasant women by a small farmer are true Hogarthian pictures" ("Charming Arminel" 4). Trevena uses suchlike comic buffoonery, exempt from tragedy, to play off against the potential misery and devastation in the lives of the principal characters.

It has been observed flippantly that what Charlotte Brontë's heroine Jane Eyre ultimately gets out of her marriage to Rochester is the chance to write her autobiography. In truth, Brontë's bride has much in common with several of Trevena's newly married women; certainly it is fair to say that for Trevena's Arminel something more than upward mobility is implied by her bid to be accepted into the ranks of the squirearchy.That such a tangle of relationships should turn out happily for Arminel is only owing to Trevena's belief in some hidden beneficence in the order of things. The seedbed of this power in Tordown affairs is Miss Challacombe's antique bed at Stokey with its curiously carved Latin phrase, *Cave amicum*–"Beware of the friend." (In *Tenebrae*the narrator says "beware of them [i.e., friends]. The closer connected the friend, the greater his selfishness" [118].) At the adjoining manor house ofNorth Beer, a tragically betrayed Maria lies buried, a girl of the lower class whose sad jilting is recounted by "Aunt Cherry" the local witch. Maria was the one who may have had this sinister motto carved on furniture. Brian translates Maria's epitaph on her grave marker: "most sweet–most miserable" (*Arminel* 230). Maria's fate is a warning for Arminel, whose elopement had led her earlier to speculate: "Suppose I should find myself alone in those streets, walking up and down, up and down. . . . If you were taken from me, I wouldn't sink. And if I were to be driven, I wouldn't go the way girls are driven. You know the beautiful blue lake in Tawton quarries where we used to meet. I should go there. I should sink after all; but I should sink there!" (191-192). Like Maria, Arminel presumably has been seduced by her first love; and although, unlike Nona, her downfall will not be caused by an unmarried pregnancy, similarities set up the reader to expect the worst. But even though the Furies intend Arminel's end to be tragic, only Maria who earlier slept in the antique bed of North Beer will be consigned to destruction; for Arminel, the unexpected intervention of a *deus ex machina* turns tragedy into happiness. A parallel instance occurs in *Furze* at its end where Trevena steps in as the author, the "*deus*" of the fiction, as it were, to save Boodles from her fate and to eject Boodles's pathetic father right out of the narrative. Similarly, Arminel's original tragic intent to drown herself is now rewritten, leaving none but the jilted village maid to die in shame: "It was only Maria who was going to bathe, and nobody wants her now" (340).

The full Latin maxim from the *Sententiae* of Publilius Siro, a first century BC aphorist and playwright, is: "Beware of trusting a friend [or lover] unless you have sufficient reason." In its undivided form this might be taken as recommending trust in a true friend. And, as with Boodles in *Furze*, Arminel indeed is saved by her love: "She charms every character in the book, charms away the evil fate that sometimes befalls girls of this station in life in England; charms a young aristocrat into marrying her, charms her father-in-law into loving her, charms her husband's proud old maiden aunt into forgiving her and finally charms the reader of her exploits into believing in her, doting on her" ("Charming Arminel" 4). Of course, Arminel's charms alone do not save the day; yet perhaps they invoke the power of a*deus ex machina* who indeed does (*Arminel* 307). Her marvelous success arises from an unexpected alteration within the contrivances of a not truly capricious fortune. Happy and unhappy couples slept in the bed of Stokey; and then the frantic Arminel is placed in it: "The old bed of Stokey had held all sorts and conditions of people. Tradition suggested it had held Queen Elizabeth. It had never been burdened with anything quite so common, or half as delightful, as Arminel" (337). The bed represents a space of dynamic, interacting usages and conventions, becoming a symbol or *symbolon* of an underlying capacity for a love worthy of honor or respectto reconstruct a world of broken dreams. When the recuperative symbols of this unseen Power speak with hope and gladness to fear and alienation, then the original selfishness and sorrow suggested by the mottos at Stokey and its adjoining manor house ofNorth Beer become rewritten as the aphorism on the oak chest: "for some reason or other the initial 'C' had been omitted, or had been removed, for the motto on the oak chest read, 'Ave Amicum,' which meant something quite different, although it could not be regarded as good Latin" (56, 228).

The Old French *gentil*, "highborn, noble," is from the Latin *gentilis*, *gens*, "belonging to the same family." Behind the Victorian definition of gentility lurks those *gentle*men who do not work with their hands, which suggests complexion and fingernails ought to be important. But physical appearance is only the superficial aspect of an antiquated belief in a literally inherited superiority. What Trevena does is reverse this definition of gentility–to set worthiness apart from inherited and institutionalized values. Gentility in Trevena's fiction is intrinsic worth, only artificially related tostatusof birth and inheritance. For Trevena, the class markers that harden into social barriers that keep people apart can be transcended when a girl from the lower orders embodies authentic highborn qualities that will serve to mend a fractured society. As will also be suggested in the analysis of *Furze* thatfollows, love seems to be about "keeping faith," hence the essence of love is neither mere gratification of desire nor the comforts of money and upward social mobility. This leaves what the innocence of Shakespeare's heroines consists in: truth, beauty,and purity. Arminel becomes a foreshadowing of the adopted orphan Boodles in *Furze*, for both are girls whose parentage is socially humble, their fathers good-natured but ineffectual and low-born. And both owe a debt to Perdita-as-Flora in Shakespeare's *Winter's Tale.* Perdita's name means "lost," but the powers of "great creating nature" override her upbringing in a shepherd's cottage; and as a lower stock may conceive a nobler bud by grafting into some higher potentiality, so her innocence and love awakens and reunites the family of Leontes. As a restorer of authentic *gentilis*, all Perdita's "acts are queens" (4.4.146). Arminel too renews and opens the family to fulfillment; but Nona's fallen nature defiles and destroys any possibility of reawakening for the spiritually dead Wistmans.

"I leant upon a coppice gate," begins Thomas Hardy in "The Darkling Thrush"–a gate not to a future of "blessed Hope" but to a country of death: "The land's sharp features seemed to be/The Century's corpse outleant." As the nineteenth century's confidence in progress dwindled away and optimism for the new twentieth century remained elusive, what had earlier been taken as progress became for some a fin-de-siècle decadence–the falling off of possibilities, a literary and artistic climate of satiety and boredom, an over-ripeness and glut. Although wealth had replaced the old politically established feudal caste system and held society together with its materialized definition of status, it also tore it apart with injustice and exclusivity. But on Henham's frontier of the Canadian northwest and elsewhere in the empire, human worth took on a more populist cast. Driven in the first instance by money as a form of social survival, what nevertheless counted most in the face of life and death issues were human actions, emotions, and moral choices. As Perdita's marriage signaled the redemption of Leontes and the renewal of his dynasty, so Arminel's and Boodles's marriages become the revitalization of decaying aristocratic families with dying roots in a more-heroic past. Beeson observed:

> During the medieval and early modern era Devon was as advanced culturally and prosperous economically as most regions of England. Tin mining and wool made it important industrially and it produced figures such as Walter Raleigh, William Browne and John Ford. But this advancement was eventually put paid to by a process of centralisation which began with the Tudors and the dissolution of the monasteries. For centuries English culture centered on London has seen Devon as a rural backwater where people are unimportant or uninteresting in comparison to the landscape. In the eighteenth and nineteenth centuries an Oxbridge-educated squire and clergy class ruled over the Devon parishes like little colonial governors, building themselves grand houses and drawing their culture from the centre. (174-175)

Dartmoor specifically had lost much of its Renaissance glory during the seventeenth and eighteenth centuries, yet the bowling alley of North Beer where the admirals who defeated the Spanish Armada drank the local cider bespeaks a vitality that Dartmoor could recover, at least in its leaders, by the example (and fertility) of its women. Cuthbert's London collection of vintage furnishings ironically consists of modern fakes that contrast with the authentic antiques at his estate of North Beer that he rarely visits because he finds the place too outdated, rural, and humble. But the effect on the senior Challacombes of Arminel's marriage and procreant future becomes a pattern and symbol, as in *The Winter's Tale* when the lost is found, for the regeneration of family and society together.

As in many a work of Gothic fiction, however, there is a hidden contrast to this rejuvenation–not just the fall of Nona, but an even greater horror festering behind the respectable poverty of the Wistmans's home-life. Wistman's wife is haunted by a cold, empty room in the tumbledown rectory where she murdered her babies by wrapping them in wet towels because she supposedthere was no money to raise them. The medical doctor was too much a quack to recognize her serial murders. This horror of the multiple infanticides returns later in *Furze* when Thomasine's "little skeletons of thought" (328, 340) assume their material incarnation in the damply dark garden and its polluted well into which her babies are dumped. This is the rock-bottom horror of "family," and we know that Nona's child likewise has no future. But after Miss Challicombe's fundamental humanity overtakes her backward-looking pride,Arminel's childwill have. Yet the flip side of Dartmoor society's return to life is this deadly,heartless insensitivity,ignorance, outright avarice, and guilty silence.

CHAPTER 6

FURZE THE CRUEL (1907)

In his epigraph to *Furze the Cruel*, the first of a proposed trilogy of novels, Trevena announced his intention of selecting for each novel a single trait in nature and locating that elemental force in his human characters: furze for cruelty, heather for endurance, and granite for strength. Rather disparagingly, a reviewer attacked this idea "of making a human being stand as the impersonation of a product of the vegetable or the mineral kingdom. . . . It is sufficiently irritating to compel a character to impersonate a particular vice or tendency, as Molière and Balzac have a way of doing, without forcing one into the yet more unnatural state of representing a quality suggested by a stone or a shrub." He doubted the remaining novels would be written, the task seemed so "formidable," and he conjectured that "perhaps Mr. Trevena will think better of it–or maybe his physician will forbid it" (Peattie, "Trevena's Cornish Story" 9). The reviewer, however, does not recognize whose fanciful aesthetics he is attacking. Presumably Trevena is taking his premise from Plato's notion in the *Phaedrus* (251b) of the "effluence" of visible surroundings to which individuals are susceptible. (Incidentally, Henham also employs this conceit in *The Feast of Bacchus*, 1907.) That ordinary humans should be influenced by nature's cruelty as much as by nymph-haunted meadows that body forth pixies like Beatrice or Petronel in *Sleeping Waters* is a form of neo-Platonism with a long history of what one should or should not behold. Hence the vicious needles of the furze become the primeval force within farmer Pendoggat of greed, lust, and cruelty that return him to the furze at the plot's climax to share its seasonal fate at swaling–a roaring conflagration. "The Furze is destroyed by fire, but grows again," says Trevena in his epigraph; even if the fiendish Pendoggat himself is permanently sidelined like the "wreck" of old furze, others will take his place.

The difference in art between the great and the pedestrian is here touched upon by a reviewer in the *Daily Mail*: "Dartmoor has inspired many good novels, but never before, we think, one quite so good as this. What it is that makes a novel great is difficult to say, but though it be a quality that we cannot define, we always know when it is present. It is in 'Furze the Cruel'–a something that makes us read without questioning the matter or the manner. . . . There is a vigorous, virile mind behind 'Furze the Cruel,' and we rest assured that Mr. Trevena will carry to a successful issue the trilogy which he has begun so well" ("Publisher's Notice," *Bracken* [ii]). Several other reviews of *Furze* are emphatic in their praise but seem unduly impressed by the harshness and repugnance of Trevena's characters:

> It may be suspected from this that the book is not pleasant reading; . . . the peasantry are sunk in ignorance, hopeless and almost incredible; their pleasures are simply sensual pleasures, and degraded at that. How can they be otherwise? Their religion and their virtues are as despicable as their vices. Farmer Pendoggat, deacon at his chapel, the murderer of his own illegitimate children, seducer of women, and betrayer of his friends, is drawn too surely and consistently not to have some living prototype. He is a real person, a living inhuman being. Taken from life, too, we are confident, are the half-witted Mary and Peter Tavy, the minister, and the old schoolmaster as ignorant as his pupils, and Thomasine, Pendoggat's victim. And as a contrast to these what does Mr. Trevena offer us? A chivalrous, almost Quixotic boy, whose chivalry is not appreciated by his parents, and a girl, whose unknown origin is an effectual bar–in the present book at any rate–to any happiness. Whether Mr. Trevena will succeed in building any happiness on this slender foundation in the two other volumes of this trilogy remains to be seen. ("Fiction," *Academy* 66-68).

And next:

> This is not one of the books which may be easily read and as easily forgotten. The heavy fragrance of the gorse remains in the nostrils; the chuckling of the Tavy as it leaps round the tors rings in the ear, and the wild moorland fills the eye long after the pages are closed; while above and beyond the fateful setting runs a story full of emotion. Idyllic episodes, realistic passages which chill the blood, and chapters of humour, are abundant. The characters live and move, and are so nicely balanced in their relations as to make them seem the result of their environment. But when Mr. Trevena shows behind the fair exterior of the country-side the human fiendishness, he

> hardly attracts people "back to the land." Perchance in the succeeding numbers of the proposed trilogy (of which this is the first, to be completed with 'Heather' and 'Granite') more alluring visions may draw us. No such thoughts as these need, however, spoil our pleasure in a powerful story ("Fiction," *Athenæum* 683-684).

Despite Trevena's encompassingly satiric style with its unsympatheticironies, few writers are more personally invested than Trevena when he presents Dartmoor's inhumanity to Brightly and Ju or describes Weevil's refusal to surrender to the Brute. Every era lashing out at the vices and follies of mankind has its own style; and the more characteristic of its time, the more untoward it seems. As Trevena integrates such literary symbols as the rebirth of nature or spirit with local details, the overriding impression in *Furze* is of that lacerating and fierce indignation of the satirist toward a sanctimonious Christianity and a self-serving heathenism, equally despicable. When that sibling odd-couple, Peter the bantam-weight and Mary the giantess, swallow their peas and plant their pills or, somewhat later, when Peter finds Chegwidden drunk and knocked unconscious on the moor, the topsy-turvy world of the quick and the dead reaches acerbic levels. These farcical moments parody parables such as the Good Samaritan or biblical miracles such as the raisings up of Jairus's daughter and of Lazarus. Whether these and other incidents in *Furze* strike the critic as tedious anecdotes, empty farces, or as a vision of the human condition through the eyes of one's fellow creature, depends on the reader's perception that whatever has been an authentic human event remains vital, that *l'humain reste humain.* Take the long scenes of Weevil's confused lying to Mr. Bellamie (a noble name in Devon) about Boodles's parentage and its even-more-confused repetition when he goes through the whole invention again with Boodles–are these scenes in which comedy falls flat or pathos sinks into bathos? Although neither truly comic nor pitiful, might not these episodes invoke a more detached, rational, and broader censure of measuring human worth by genteel standards? If so, their generic foozling is owing to the author's angry questioning of an injurious class system, an attack more subtle than the novel's direct satirizing of the villagers' drunkenness, hypocrisy, or cruelty to animals and each other.

Frederic Cooper seems almost baffled by the thematic structure of *Furze*: it "is not a book which profits by a minute analysis of plot. There are a score of tangled threads of destiny, crossing and recrossing. . . . It is one of those books that are spread over a wide canvas; . . . there is no one man or woman in it whom you may single out as the central figure" (335). Cooper is thinking of those plots that bring details together in a seamless sequence, one incident causing or leading to the next, as the reader enjoys a growing understanding of the developing conflict. But *Furze* is less dependent on plot than on theme and image; its incidents initially seem to have little or no cause-and-effect relationship. Although Cooper is too well-read to believe that this is a defectively constructed novel, he indirectly implies the lack of an evolving unified conflict. But as in the Romantic informal essay or as in George Meredith's novels the precedent for Trevena's character-packed plots existed. Trevena is among those at the turn of the last century who were taking narrative beyond conventional forms, replacing the smoothly unilinear plot with open-ended thematic analogues or contrasts, using inverted parallels, ironic juxtapositions, and a correspondingly discontinuous chronology. One such micro-juxtaposition in *Furze* is the Grandmother pixie describing evolutionary time, and Peter's Grandfather clock, patriarch of human time gone haywire. But in *Furze* the plot *does* weave the initially divergent threads of its assorted characters progressively closer. Ultimately two major strands emerge: the romance of Boodles and Aubrey in contrast to the violation of Thomasine by the lecherous Pendogget.

Furze had begun with a fairy-tale of geological evolution appropriate to the folklore of Dartmoor, a meditation on rain as the *Ur*-force in nature underlying the furze, heather, granite, and bracken. The symbolism of showers is explicated in *Raindrops* (1920) by an old geologist, Trevena's persona, who says the rain as creator and destroyer shapes and sculpts the rock. People's lives are like those raindrops. It is as if each life is one among many drops from which threads of events emerge and, from these, global dimensions are created; then beyond, a deeper reality one cannot see. Trevena himself, at the close of his career, says: "I have tried to point out that this life of ours is merely a phase, not a complete history. . . . The life of a tree or plant may be more closely associated with our own, in the way of knowledge of a kind and memory, even suffering, than we can imagine. I should like to enlarge upon this theme, but it is too late now" (Henry 18). Trevena believed plants may have "consciousness and character. . . . These wild flowers possess an inner life, about which we know as little as we do concerning our own souls" (*Adventures* 9-10, 19). Plants, says Trevena, never predictably follow the rules of horticulture; gentians will "flourish in the backyard of some poor man who occasionally tramples upon them with his hobnailed boots; while in the pleasance of a reigning duke, served leaf and root by gorgeous flunkeys, with all appliances and means to flower, each plant remains as blind as Bartimæus"–whose sight could be restored only by miracle (*Adventures* 48; Mark 10:46-52). Trevena jokes that anemones will not grow for him because he is Judas: "I fear that little transaction of childhood, when I betrayed sixty innocent blooms of the Pasque Flower into the hands of a botanist, for the same number of shillings, has never been forgiven" (*Adventures* 10). Nature's is a life of lurking possibilities, comfortable even with such interwoven gender constructionsas that of Aubrey, whom Boodles repeatedly describes as a boy with a girl's face, or that of Mary, the good-hearted hermaphrodite more powerful than any male. Likewise, Mary's fondness for Old Sal, the rebarbative twenty-two year old goose, is no less an affinity of nature than that of Brightly for Ju, or Weevil for the pixy Boodles. And Boodles as an emerging sprite of nature is far less locked into the binary and essentialist role of gender norms than is Thomasine.

Among the first characters introduced in *Furze* is Brightly, a trader in rabbit-skins–totally poor, intellectually weak, an innocent who struggles to rise above the working-class prejudice against the homeless. Tanguyreports that "an appeal for the pedler Brightly was inserted in some copies of *Furze the Cruel*, which proves that the old purveyor of rabbit skins actually existed" (113). At a revival service Brightly hears "Jerusalem the Golden" which becomes such an icon to his yearning soul that he names his companion dog "Ju." Brightly's ironic vision, the *urbs Sion aurea* of Revelation 21:18 originated in Bernard of Cluny's long poem "*De Contemptu Mundi*" (c.1140). Its nineteenth-century English translator pointed out that the poem was "a bitter satire on the fearful corruptions of the age. But as a contrast to the misery and pollution of the earth, the poem opens with a description of the peace and glory of heaven, of such rare beauty as not easily to be matched by any medieval composition on the same theme" (Morrison 55). Brightly and Ju are quest figures, wandering, lost in "misery and pollution," never to arrive at "peace and glory." Trevena's white-hot anger against those who are cruel to the helpless emerges in his description of society's treatment of these two who are victims of the Brute–Brightly because he is severely slow-witted, Ju because she is a dog without a license.

Abel Cain Weevil, Boodles's step-father, is a paralyzed figure, an ineffectual and failed animal-rights polemicist. His given names recall Adam's sons–Abel, the first murder victim, and Cain, the first murderer. As brothers, the victim and the originator of evil suggest for Abel-Cain a schizoid sense of shame, the inability to claim his own psychological space and a paradoxical longing both for human companionship and for escape from membership in the human race. As to Weevil's surname, it refers to a pest that unobtrusively destroys young plants, eating new growth such as young buds and fruits–in short, given Trevena's love of flowers, it suggests a sense of self-guilt and implicit punishment. His countrymen don't know what to make of a man who talks to animals and raises a child not his own. They think he is an idiot or a mentally ill loner, but in reality his reclusiveness has created an inner connection to creaturely experience, a kinship with all life. Sensitive to pain, animals are yet condemned to dwell without the symbols of illusion or hope, and Weevil feels a kinship with them. Trevena insists in *Furze* that "Those animals, such as the horse and dog, who have been brought up with men, and acquired so much from them, have an equal right to be protected by the laws which protect men" (183). Apropos of such as Ju, Trevena writes: "I have tried to point out . . . that we human beings are perhaps inclined to rate ourselves too high above the animals" (Henry 2). At another point, Trevena says it is good Boodles did not see the animal market as it might "have reminded her that, for some cause unexplained, the dominant note of all things is cruelty; from the height of the unknown God, who gives His beings a short life and scourges them through it, to the depth of the invisible mite who rends a still smaller mite in pieces" (*Furze* 142). In *Adventures Among Wild Flowers,* Trevena writes that Shakespeare, "who knew man and his nature so well, could not observe the animals. He loathed the dog–that cannot be forgiven him–regarded the owl as 'fiendish,' and directed all his adjectives of malevolence against 'the full blown toad that venom spits'" (258-259).

Boodles's frequent depicting of herself as only an innocent child may be her pixy persona or, contrawise, a coy hint that she actually is more than a passive child and that her innocence and goodness does not lack power, as perhaps her awareness of Psalm 8 suggests. A pixy-like foundling, Boodles's name derives from "booty," a West Country way of pronouncing "beauty." Her lack of ancestry or "birth," as a baby left wrapped in fern with barely any identity but life itself, seems almost a nod to T.E. Brown's tale, "Christmas Rose" in *Fo'c's'le Yarns*, that similarly describes a mysterious girl of elemental nature, a child rescued from shipwreck, born of the sea, rejoicing in stormy weather, and killed by lightening with flowers in her hands and hair. All we know for sure about the identity of Brown's mythologic girl is the ship's name, Hidalgo, "noble," and the arms and cipher on her gown, the latter signifying *Imperatoris Domus* or "royal household," used with the heraldic device by Spanish royalty. For Boodles, her lack of "birth" and "name" becomes the occasion for her nobler reincarnation as the goddess Flora. Aubrey "had never met any girl with a tithe of her wonderful spring-like freshness, which suggested the sweet earth covered with flowers and steaming after a shower of warm rain. Boodles seemed to him to be composed of this warm earth, sunshine and rain, with the beauty and sweetness of the flowers added" (*Furze* 247). Her connection with the primary powers of nature is reinforced by analogy with the proud river Tavy that, like Boodles, also does not know its source, only that it begins somewhere near Cranmere pool.

Boodles's closeness to nature is in contrast to the harmful class consciousness of the Bellamies who, in effect, are "fighting against Nature" (324). Aubrey's father thinks in aesthetic terms, much like the preciosity of Oscar Wilde's Dorian Gray or Lord Henry Wotton. Although Mr. Bellamie's inhibited wife also endorses bourgeois values, Mrs. Bellamie recalls she was once nearly as poor as Boodles. Mr. Bellamie (*quasi bella et amabilis*) seems to have inherited the gentrified *bella* part of his surname without its empathetic *amie*, which seems a bit more applicable to his wife. Because Boodles will not marry Aubrey without his father's consent, she very nearly destroys her happiness by binding herself to socially constructed imperatives. Although she will not attempt the pathetic prevarications of Weevil, she too rehearses a white lie. Her capitulation to class sensibility is no less a fall from her original innocence and goodness than were Weevil's betrayals of the truth. At this point Boodles's romance with Aubrey can turn either into a tragedy or blossom into lasting happiness. Trevena sets up the reader's expectations for the worst–then with a god-like smile he relents and chooses the happy ending. Only Aubrey's chivalrous love, slaying the gorgon of parental consent, of considerations of property and status, gives back to Boodles her innocence and sets her entirely free of social pressures. She gets her prince, who fully exemplifies the meaning of his surname, "beauty and love."

Oddly, Lewis Melville seems to have selected Thomasine, not Boodles, as the story's heroine–which she probably would have been in anĖmile Zola novel. Trevena's Thomasine is as innocent as Boodles and almost as generous to Brightly. But she is Boodles lost, Boodles without her transforming imagination: "The life of the soul was in the eyes of Boodles; the life of the body in Thomasine's" (148). This division of soul's beauty and body's beauty is a familiar duality that portrays women as either divine or earthy. Trevena knows masculine desire is complicitous in projecting one or the other extreme upon the woman. Thomasine is no conscious temptress but one whose beauty and dim-witted ignorance cause her to become the victim of her own sexuality, helplessly caught in the mind-forged manacles (William Blake's figure) of her social and mental backwardness: "It is not pleasant to see a pretty face, glorious complexion, well-made body, without mind, intellect, or soul worth mentioning; but it is a common sight" (62). The villainous seducer Pendoggat, who takes her from her suitor, snarls at Thomasine: "'You're mine, blood and flesh, and all that's in you, and I'll have you or die for it.' . . . While speaking he was half dragging her towards the ruined miner's cot, and there flung her savagely on the fern" (100). His rape makes her a fallen woman, and "the opportunity of leading a respectable life had gone from her, like her sweetheart, never to return" (175).

The single point of direct contact between the contrasting couples of Boodles and Aubrey, Thomasine and Pendogget, occurs at the story's end when Boodles unwittingly but with poetic justice burns the villainous Pendoggat in the furze: "It was a mighty brake, twenty years untouched, and there were no flowers upon it. The interior was a choked mass of dead growth" (302). Botanically, this is very much the opposite of Boodles's springtime embodiment of nature. In the Prologue to *Furze* Trevena had written that "the Furze is destroyed by fire, but grows again." Itsreturn is a sinister token of the ineradicable persistence of cruelty. Indeed, says F. T. Cooper, the furze:

> as the incarnate symbol of the spirit of cruelty in nature and in man . . . defies extermination; that, no matter how you hack and dig and burn its roots, springs up again, grim and indomitable; and if the chief characters in the book are morally warped and misshapen, it is because they, too, have sprung from the soil which gives birth to the Furze; and when, in the end, Pendoggat, the cruelest, thorniest man of them all, meets a hideous fate, it is no small tribute to the crude force of the story to say that one feels there is a certain symbolic justice that he should receive his punishment through the instrumentality of the Furze itself. (335-336)

And, of course, Pendoggat had preached hell fire as the final end for everyone but himself–although "he had become horribly afraid of fire since Peter made the mommet" (343):

> The hideous picture of Pendoggat, miser, coward, thief, without one tender, redeeming trait, one vestige of a moral sense, caught at last in the very center of a huge clump of burning furze, struggling and writhing in its tangles like a wild beast, torn and scarred by its briars, and finally feeling the blasting breath of the flames roll past to leave him a quivering, blackened, blinded thing, still grasping in his helpless fingers the ashes of the fortune for which he had sinned, recalls . . .

—and here Cooper cites a figure from Frank Norris's *Octopus* (336). But I would prefer to say that this more appropriately invokes Dante's Inferno in all its figurative import. Was not this also the very place where Pendoggat's own illegitimate babies lay murdered by him, the very *cor corum* of his criminality? And it is worth noting, on a less epic level, that Pendoggat, who killed Mary's old goose, had buried it in just that furze where he was burned–Sal is fully avenged too.

In the last phase of the story Boodles has reconciled herself to accepting a companion in lieu of marriage, a woman to "sleep with her" (*Furze* 385). But even Mary Tavy knows "It bain't a maid yew wants, my dear, but the butiful young gentleman" (383). Then when Aubrey kisses her, it becomes "just as if the story was going to end, not in the second best way, but in the most blissful manner possible, with a dance of fairies on Tavy banks and a wedding-march" (388). The deterministic curses of heredity and environment that make Boodles the Beast's helpless victim are annulled. This is "the proper ending of the story, the ending that the gods had written in their manuscript and the compositor-ogres had tried to mar in their wicked way" (386):

> The past was to vanish, not as if it had never been, but because it really never had been. The story was to begin all over again, as the other one had been conceived so badly that nobody could stand it. The once upon a time stage had come again, and the ogres had agreed not to interfere this time. Boodles baptised herself in dew, and rose from the ceremony only a few hours old. The child's name was Flora; no connection of the poor little thing which had been flung out to perish because nobody wanted it except silly old Weevil, who hated to see animals hurt. Weevil belonged to the other story too, the rejected story, and therefore he had never existed. Nobody had wanted Boodles, which was natural enough, as she was merely a wretched illegitimate brat; but every one wanted Flora. The world would be a dreary place without its flowers. Flora could laugh Mr. Bellamie to scorn; for the sun was her father and the warm earth her mother; and nobody would stop to look at the flowers while she was going by with them all upon her face. (387)

By invoking the magic of a god-like authorial hand that composes the story's true ending, Trevena prevents his readers from mentally acceding to the inevitability of the Brute's purely social and economic power which had seemed, to both author and reader alike, so real and inescapable. Literary naturalism or material determinism might try to label this the uplifting view of a pious "Victorianism," but the author's strategy is to forefend the promised end by enlisting the folklore of Dartmoor as a counter-force that will not allow the manacles of the Brute to exercise absolute authority over the story's outcome.

Trevena's magical counter-force invokes the symbol as found in Romantic and post-Romantic literature. Critics long have recognized that Romantic writers, despite their devotion to "humble and rustic life" in which "the essential passions of the heart find a better soil" when "incorporated with the beautiful and permanent forms of nature" (Wordsworth 734-735), are yet threatened by dark and painful interludes. Although the Romantics speak of the symbol's "translucence" or define it as "transparent," promising direct access to some metaphysical plenitude or "blue flower" of pure Truth, this is qualified by the fact that their dream-fantasies often waver, dissolve, and turn the seeker back upon a darker double. Their irresolute quest thus entertains an illusion of a direct transcendental access that the seeker experiences as delusive; yet that aspiration is what props up or nourishes daily life. One needs illusions to live in the real world successfully, even while knowing that they cannot literally be true. The question then remains, in what other way might they be true? To pinpoint this symbolism of hope in *Furze*, one should begin by considering the homeless Brightly and the illegitimate Boodles in terms of Trevena's recurrent image of the gate-as-threshold. Brightly will never escape, figuratively speaking, the rubbish heap on which he sits by the gate. But by virtue of her existence on the social threshold or margin where behavioral codes are provisionally held in abeyance, Boodles can more clearly see and challenge the worlds from which she is excluded, growing to understand alternative possibilities for herself.

Once closed, neither the gate to fairyland nor to genteel domesticity can be reopened by mere force of her desire. Boodles's predicament is archetypally prefigured in Adam and Eve's lost innocence and expulsion from Eden. Their status is irrevocably changed–but changed so that they re-emerge with enhanced dignity, inasmuch as Milton's Archangel Michael promises Adam "a paradise within thee, happier far" (12:582). As Boodles hovers on the threshold of Eve's knowledge, she too undergoes a similar *felix culpa* in her personal development that produces a new knowledge of sorrow and happiness, reality and imagination, falsehood and truth, tragedy and joy. The blue flowers of the saxifrage and the forget-me-not, "which not only restored sight to the blind, but life also to the dead" (*Furze* 11), become Trevena's symbols of her paradise regained. The saxifrages, called stone-breakers (from L. *saxum*, rock + *frangere*, to break), thrive in fissures of rocks, seemingly splitting them through bio-erosion. But in *Adventures with Wild Flowers* Trevena says that in "the great myth of the saxifrage" it would be a mistake to imagine "a plant with roots sufficiently strong to split the hardest rocks" (292, 297). He believes the saxifrage opportunistically seizes upon crevices and its blue flowers are symbols of something far more deeply interfused (Wordsworth's phrase). The difference between splitting the rock for its own benefit and turning to account an already existing crevice is the same difference as that between a diabolic breaking and a symbolic healing, enabling the self to see the external world as that in which its greatest happiness consists. The blue flower is that renewed harmony within a fractured world, an echo of the primal unity of the Garden, archetype of all Trevena's personal gardens.

Like Arminel, Boodles also marries into the gentry. The ring Aubrey gave to Boodles "with the blue forget-me-nots" fulfills at the conclusion its mawkish motto, "Love me and leave me not" (*Furze,* 246). It is a sweet sentiment but typical of Aubrey's conventional intellect, loyal but lacking edge brilliance of personality. Boodles's happiness is not because she has married a man of educational and intellectual distinction, nor because she has broken the class barrier and is now about to lead the comfortable life of the gentry. For her, rather, happiness is the validation of her humanity, a pairing of emotional coequals, heart to proportionate heart. Charlotte Bronte's Jane Eyre observed: "I am my husband's life as fully as he is mine. . . . To be together is for us to be at once as free as in solitude, as gay as in company. . . . We are precisely suited in character—perfect concord is the result" (Chapter 38). To be human is to accept the inequities of nature and circumstance; but to be in love is to employ sorrows and disappointments against themselves to summon into being a simulacrum of the remembered fairyland. Fairyland may contain much that Boodles and Aubrey have lost or never had; but the implication here is that perhaps Boodles and Aubrey may be "happier far."

Still, one would like to be able to ask John Trevena over a glass of his excellent brandy about the sad or happy alternatives to his story's conclusion, about the chilliness of reality seeping in as it did with the open-ended possibilities in Charles Dickens's*Great Expectations*. George Bernard Shaw felt Dickens' novel was too serious a book to be a trivially happy one. Its beginning and middle was unhappy, so the conventional happy ending was an outrage upon it. One would like to ask Trevena if he envisioned a new role for the pagan fairies of the Gaels and the happy endings of ancient legends, no less magical perhaps when "the goddess of love became a Madonna" and "the sun-temple was turned into a church" (*Furze* 72). Might, perhaps, Trevena say that both possible outcomes in *Furze* are plausible but that the reader must draw from his inmost perceptions of the sacred and profane the justification for one over the other. But, as Trevena once wistfully remarked, "We are not to meet personally, yet we cannot pass as strangers, for the intimate condition of speaker and listener is established between us. It is one of the sorrows of an author's life, that he cannot meet those who appreciate his writings, because they are exactly the people he was meant to know" (*Adventures* 12).

CHAPTER 7

HEATHER (1908) | *GRANITE* (1909)

The people that populate *Furze the Cruel* are throughout entirely Dartmoor locals, and the novel's mysticism, if not its superstition, is restrained. In each of following two novels,a subtle mysticism becomesan increasingly significant factor. Later in *Bracken* Trevena uses "moorland symbolism" but introduces neither the rustics nor their Devonshire dialect. *Bracken*, we may say, is the mystical capstone that transforms the previous three novels into a tetralogy. This increasing tilt of characterization towards mysticism across Trevena's entire landscape is supported by his tendency to sidestepthe local mining or farming activities of commercial Dartmoor. With the exception of old Will Yeo's stonebreaking in *Granite* (or such scenes elsewhere as Mary Tavy forking manure or Thirza Billacott sorting potatoes) Trevena's novels do not dwell as do Hardy's, for example,on the particulars of agricultural implements. The natives are largely seen at home, tavern, market or, like Willum Cobbledick, loafing about. Actual local activities such as Goose Fair in *Furze* or the cider tasting contest in *Sleeping Waters* become nodes for Trevena's social commentary and, more generally, so too do figures of the squirearchy, hypocrites of the law and established religion, and the natives' drunkenness and cruelty to animals. Also in each of the following narratives, Trevena customarily includes a male and/or female who are what the moor folk would call "foreigners"–semi-autobiographical outsiders, many of whom have come to the moor for purposes of regaining their health–or others locally born but raised so that they stand apart from those rooted in the community: Burrough and Beatrice in *Pixy*, Brian and the eponymous Arminel, Boodles in *Furze*, Brunscombe in *Heather,* Anger and Petronel in *Sleeping Waters*. Mark Yeo in *Granite*,for instance, was born in Fursdon (as opposed to simply "found" like Boodles) but exfiltrated back from Canada with an outsider's perspective.

Heather

In his epigraph to *Furze the Cruel,* Trevena wrote that the heather on the moor "is torn by winds, but blossoms again" because of its "endurance." The opening scene in this next novel is on a hill-top with a neolithic grave or "kistvaen" among the heather. The internal thoughts of George Brunacombe, the novel's protagonist, are presented as an externalized voice from this ancient tomb. Trevena imagines the *Siste, viator* or "stop, traveler" of ancient Roman roadside tombs giving voice not just to the deceased but also to the passersby in whose minds those words now are heard and who internalize for a moment the deceased's destiny. This voice reminds George of his mortality but gives no answer to his murky future. Then Trevena's dramatization of human mortality moves narratively to the patients at a tuberculosis sanatorium. Who will be destroyed by the disease, and who will endure to "blossom again"? This contrasts with a psychological and figurative dimension from nineteenth-century novels and operas. The metaphors of tuberculosis turned the bodily syndrome into a mythology of the Romantic personality, expressing nobility, creativity, melancholia, or wistfulness. Trevena's more modern sense is that the physical symptoms are environmental and treatable, although he does apparently endorse a bit of the old mythology of illness: "Genius is certainly madness, and inspiration a form of ill-health" (*Heather* 122). As in *The Magic Mountain* (1924), Thomas Mann's philosophical novel of an isolated tuberculosis sanatorium in the mountains, the patients become a microcosm for the spiritual and psychological illnesses of society at large. Trevena's concern with humanity's actuating conditions, those influences of the milieu, focuses his social critique here on drunkenness, abuse of women, and forces at large in the world such as self-indulgent materialism. For example, Richard Halfacre, a nihilistic socialist like Joseph Conrad's bomb-throwing terrorist in *The Secret Agent* (1907), oafishly attacked all institutions, and so at the end of the narrative he is permanently incarcerated where he needs to be–in a mental asylum.

Elia Peattie says Trevena's *Heather* deserves "the respectful consideration of those who complain that there are no masters of fiction arising to comfort us for the going of men like Meredith. Mr. Trevena . . . will always stand high above the applause of those who must be easily amused. He will escape popularity in the more tawdry meaning of the word" (Peattie, "Second . . ." 12). The heather, silent and visible, and the wind, noisy and invisible, are cast as adversaries–the wind tearing the heather, the heather unbeaten by the wind. A*New York Times* reviewer nailed the analogy: "As the seemingly fragile heather defies the moorland winds, so does human nature seem to survive shocks which seem fatal in prospective. . . . The boisterous weather is glorified until it becomes the very spirit and atmosphere of the tale, and all the people who move in it are . . . creatures of the heather and the wind . . . and they cannot live elsewhere" ("Spirit of Endurance" BR366). Pushing his airy analogy even further, Trevena also envisions the wind as like the universal Mind.Beginning in miracle at the origin of life, it "beats through the bodies of men from somewhere and passes on" (6), very much one might add, as Percy Shelley's "Power" does in his poem "Mont Blanc." Just like the wind tearing through the heather in the phenomenal world, so the Mind's forward-pushing *élan vital* burdens happiness with thoughts of mortality; but by the mystery of the present moment'sreach into reality as a whole,mankind is given the power to resist, endure, and perhaps find joy.

Heather's protagonist, George Brunacombe, who has left London to recover his health on the moor, lives with a one-legged owl in an old house annexed to an abandoned copper mine, painting and writing in "cursed loneliness." Setting aside Trevena'scaricatured autobiography in *The Dartmoor House that Jack Built*, probably the author's most comprehensive self-portrait is George here in *Heather*, though whether this is an artistically smartened portrayal or closer to real life one cannot tell. But Trevena did mentionhis selling of "engravings," as George does paintings, to survive while writing and awaiting the publication of *Pixy* ("John Trevena"106). George's surname Brunacombe is Old English and Celtic, compounded from either *Bran* or *Brun* (brown) and *cwm* (steep-sided valley), deriving in its variant spellings from the Roman British era, specifically from the village of Branscombe in East Devon. As an artist working hard to produce canvases for a living, George perhaps should be combined with Trevena's portrayal of the classical scholar John Burrough in *A Pixy in Petticoats*. For George, Winnie Shazell, the novel's heroine, is the girl of his dreams; and like her, George also is "a fragile growth tormented with disease" (*Heather* 277). Winnie had been born on the moor and was unable to live away from it. She had moved with her family to the city and nearly dies of tuberculosis working at a postal sub-station within a squalid grocery store. Her name is from Saint Winifred who, because of her oath to remain chaste, is the patron of virgins; hardly coincidentally, there is a Saint Winifred's Church in Branscombe. Winnie, engaged to Ernest Hawker who pays her hospitalization but whom she does not love, is the most ill of the patients at the Sanatorium. Her middle name, Erica, invokes the heather family of *Ericaceae*: "Like her they were fragile but they bore the rough life, and more, they could hardly exist without it. . . . The roses would drop their petals and be dead in a day; but the heather is a thing that endures" (88). As to Winnie's destiny, she first marries the tyrannical socialist Halfacre and is dragged to London where she relapses, then later almost dies by the sea in Cornwall, and finally is rescued by George to live with him on the moor.

The reviewer at New York's *Evening Post* seemed unhappy with the characters as drawn, describing the sanatorium as "an institution that . . . savors strongly of an asylum for the insane" and asserting that among all the characters "only three are represented with a thoroughly sane and healthy outlook on life–Gregory Breakback, the clean-hearted peasant visionary; Tobias, the fox-terrier; and Bubo, the one-legged owl" ("Current Fiction"7). George's friend, Gregory Breakback, the sixty-two year old granite-breaker with his long rod of iron, so very symbolic of his rectitude, is indeed among the most sane and surely the most chaste of Dartmoor's rustics. Several of Trevena's novels if written as theatrical dramas could be performed on the boards, not just read in the "closet"; and in *Heather* especially the residents of the sanatorium are a self-revealing cast of characters. With a stage and a wind machine, they could put on a fine Ibsen-like performance, marital issues and all. This also includes the thespian qualities of the local rustics–primordial Calabans, staggering drunk in the fields like the stones Pyrrha and Deucalion threw over their shoulders when Zeus ended the Age of Bronze. Perhaps one of Winnie's sanatorium friends, Berenice, "the girl who would have been a man" (288), is among the most dramatizeable of characters.

Her sexuality is partly environmental and partly genetic: "There was nothing vile about her. Her affections had simply wandered away into unusual channels and her vision had become distorted, partly by her physical condition, partly by encouraging unnatural sympathies. Nature must have played some trick with her temperament at the beginning, just as she does with potatoes, making one tuber forked like a man and another featured like a monkey" (260). She ends her life in love with her adopted dog Tobias. A fable of Aesop applies to Berenice and Winnie: "the only growth that will not break is the one that bends" (472). Berenice dies, Winnie lives: "the stiff growth had been snapped off, the clinging one lived on" (467). Winnie fancifully bends a "stalk of heather" about her finger for her fairy-dance marriage ceremony to George (476).

Of course, as theater, one would have to prune somewhat Trevena's rich accounts of nature, folklore, and history. One very long "digression" about the thirteenth-century Perambulators delimiting the boundaries of the Forest of Dartmoor describes in such lovingly circumstantial detail the path of these knightly surveyors that only a passionate hiker or a life-long resident could pleasurably visualize–very much as if the author himself had retraced this topographical and historical circuit. But as in *Furze the Cruel*, the plot's threads of relationships knit slowly into a jigsaw pattern of powerful dimensions. What contemporary readers must recognize is that this historic delimitation (the Forest is *in* Dartmore, not identical with it) is all about ancient property rights–and the present-day exclusive authority of the commoners to use its resources. "Dartmoor folk have often shown that they are in some senses outside the law of the land; they rely on their own rights and strength, which outsiders must have a giant's power to break down. They will part with nothing, they have withstood the Duchy officials with complete success" (320). Although Dartmoor was nominally under the control of the Duke of Cornwall, the "giant's power" traditionally belonged to the sharing group of commoners who had no incentive to monitor Dartmoor's resources. Destruction of neolithic remains for construction and road repair was certainly one outrageous abuse. The legal use of other stones for granite "hedges," the cutting of peat, the grazing of sheep, cattle, or horses, and the illegal enclosing sections of the land for private use–all this had been nebulously regulated.

But the old "giant's power" was of the past; "the age of cunning has begun; and God help the giant" (29). So "little Mr. Odyorne," the paralegal, plots a devious net in which to ensnare the local Pethericks. His name, originally "Hodierne" from the Latin contractions of *hoc/hic dies,*"this day," as in our obsolete "hodiernal," is the characternym for a cunningly successful opportunist. Similarly, the local rector and Trevena's blackest clergyman, Francis Leigh, secretly employed arson and fraud to evict his tenants rather than respond to their expensive requests to repair his cottages. He *parsonally* burns down half the hovels in the village for the insurance but is, ironically, seen as a "good and ardent churchman" (422). Commenting on the failure of the cottagers to win better shelter from their Rector, Trevena recalls from Joseph Jacobs's *English Fairy Tales* (1890) the story of the native Cornishman, "Jack the Giant-Killer": "The whole matter resolved itself into a political struggle; and politics change the condition of a country slowly. In the battle between brain and muscle, in an age of cunning, brain wins; for muscle is the foolish giant of fairy-stories, believing everything that it is told, and stabbing itself with the carving-knife that it may see the pease-pudding tumbling out of its stomach; and brain is the tricky mischievous sprite, the Jack of the stories, dodging up and down with sword and lantern, stabbing and burning heedless of consequences" (201-202).Halfacre the Socialist "supposed this giant could be revived and given a mad political kind of strength; not asking himself what affinity there could be between the plain man of intellect who devoted all that was in him to his art . . . and the beer-swilling lout whose ambition it is to do no work at all" (376). Halfacre is so devoid of common sense that even seasoned philosophers understand his goals no better than did the simple-minded John Petherick.

Trevena caricatures this striving for personal advantage in an unforgettably morbid vignette of the commoners competing for a burial site. The lazy sexton had cut down a fast-growing tree in the nook between the church's wall and its porch, opening a wonderfully well-positioned new plot in the crowded graveyard. When the Rector allocates it to whoever dies next, this unleashes an unseemly contest among the oldsters to gain the coveted site by dying first–a competition as godless as that of Robert Browning's

Bishop and old Gandolf. The ironic winner is the boyish and drunken John Petherick, whom Father hit on the noggin with a coal-hammer causing fits of dizziness followed by John falling conclusively on his head (439). His fat widow gets drunk at his funeral, "clambered upon the table, fell among the meat and drink, got to her feet, pulled her clothes up, and danced, a shocking and shameless sight to the pure sunshine" (450). We suppose that stays and corsets needed no dress reform on Dartmoor by reason of their non-existence and that undergarments, massproduced or otherwise, had never been part of her wardrobe. All of this is in counterpoint to the desperate cheerfulness of the sanatorium patients, locked almost allegorically in a *danse macabre* with the inevitability of their deaths, likely sooner than later. Trevena's vignette puts one in mind of the parable of Leo Tolstoy, the Russian nobleman turned Christian mystic, "How Much Land Does a Man Need?" (1886). And as well, perhaps, of Anton Chekov's comment: "It is a common saying that a man needs only six feet of earth. But six feet is what a corpse needs, not a man. Man needs not six feet of earth, not a farm, but the whole globe, all of nature, where unhindered he can display all the capacities and peculiarities of his free spirit." That puts the commoners' competition for the consecratedcorner in perspective.

At Christmas, George poses questions for the Rector about his belief in an afterlife: "'My creed is, "I believe in a Creator, who made you, me, and everything, amen." Not a syllable more. Isn't yours the same? You're a sane man. You're a clever man,' he cried bitterly. 'Do you believe that those bones on the other side of the hedge yonder will creep out of their holes one day, and put the same flesh on them, and be the same slouching folk?'" (341). As George leaves, both men see a procession of ghostly medieval nuns. Leigh exclaims:

> "You saw them too. We both saw them at the same moment."
> "Liver," said George stubbornly.
> "Six," Leigh muttered.
> "Seven. One walked in front."
> "They swayed from side to side. Not a sound. No chanting," Leigh panted.
> "All in black, and those big hoods. One of 'em limped."
> "The last bearer on the right. When they came round the curve

> in the path I noticed it. They walked in step. They swayed from side to side."
> "Bah," said George. "It was a nightmare. We want some medicine."
> "I didn't see the coffin."
> "There wouldn't be one–at that period."
> "I saw no body."
> "Nor I."
> "Why didn't we? Where was it?" (346)

It is a "mystery which had some unattainable truth at the bottom of it" (408). Leigh tells George afterwards that the nuns "went across the week after you saw them, then twice a week, and now every evening just as it gets dark, swaying from side to side" (421). The procession, awaiting its corpse, reminds Leigh that it is his fate to be torn from life at any moment, but he cannot find the courage to face this abhorrent reality. Leigh tries to exorcize the procession but to no avail. Although for him belief in the immortality of the soul is impossible, Leigh tries to disguise his anxiety of death both by refusing to question the Church of England's preachments on the afterlife and by simultaneously smothering in religious ritual any insights about the mystery and struggles of life. He devotes himself heart and mind to rose cultivation, escaping very ironically into life as a garden of roses. His wife has run off to a cripplingly expensive foreign affair; and he has made the cook/housekeeper his mistress.

After George recovers the profits of his art out of which he had been cheated by a dealer of a questionable sort, the power of wealth is now his. Although in anger George stereotypes the dealer negatively, the merchant's background is incidental to his role in disguising or eliminating a troublesome reality from the other side of the artist's spiritual relationship with the timeless forces of nature–the pursuit of profit by means of artistic creation. Since George was originally working under the impression that his art was of little commercial value, the dealer sanitized or absolved him from the urban marketplace and the aggressive materialism at the root of his new wealth. George's art dealer is by no means the most unethical of figures in the novel: very much worse are Francis Leigh who burnt the village for insurance and "couldn't tell right from wrong" (422), or Odyorne who schemes to deprive the commoners of their property, or Halfacre as a would-be bomb-throwing wife-abuser who locks Winnie and her mother in a room and suffers from a paranoid persecution complex. But irked at being cheated, George entirely overlooks the pivotal role his agent played in the pursuit of profit–by building a critical reception for his art with an "exhibition" that "made you a big man" (417-18). Most significantly, George's sudden discovery of artistic success leads to self-affirmation, giving him the backbone to take hold of and to control his destiny.

In a shop window in Plymouth, Winnie catches sight of a picture by George entitled "Lost," a scene of "the Ford, and she herself was about to cross, but lingering and afraid, because she did not know what awaited her on the other side" (381). Her former fellow patient Gumm, who indeed is dying but has capitulated, also passed the window but doesn't recognize either the Ford or Winnie herself (381)."Lost" is in contrast to George's earlier picture of the Perambulators in the moonlight "where the river moves so fast as to appear motionless, shining figures walk from among the oaks and follow each other across the Ford" (77), a "dream-picture" of knights who have determined "the boundary of the Forest" and are "near the end of their journey" (80, 86). (One of their boundary beacons still stands nearby on Cawsand, now called Cosdon.) Anything but lost, the Perambulatorshave determined by exact measurements their whereabouts, and they cross with assurance. George has had a dream: Winnie is afraid the wind will sweep her away and he hears her crying, "'I am lost'" (411). But his dreaming also furnishes him an answer: "Down the steep pathway climbed the twelve great figures in their bright mail, and they crossed the Ford one by one, gazing ahead with stern faces. They had nearly finished their journey, they had endured the storms, and were completing the task which would never be forgotten; and then each knight became a clap of thunder, rolling into the side of Cawsand with a dolorous roar, and where each man struck was a blaze of fire" (410).

Whereas the knights affirm the Alpha and Omega of eternity, the medieval nuns are the opposite of the Perambulators, ghostly shadows bearing those lost in radical despair to the grave. At that moment, in that place, George and Winnie can find in their personal endurance of the stormy wind an existential courage, similar to the literal intrepid gallantry of the Perambulators, to cross over from the ever-present threat of non-being to a thunderous encounter with the holy beyond the flaming ramparts of the world. Winnie receives medical permission in August to go down to St. Michael's Ford: "It was there they had met on the earlier stage of their perambulation; it was there they were to finish the journey, among the ghosts of those who had crossed the Ford completing their journey, settling the bounds, bringing liberty, appointing the great Forest as a free and open space for all time" (472). In a very primeval church with her ring of heather, Winnie and George embrace the miracle of finding that which she believed her life had lost:

> "Come along quick, or the doors will be shut, and St. Michael will have gone home to supper. Surely St. Michael is a good enough parson for us. Come along, Gee, to the green shelf above the waterfall, and we'll be married there."
>
> "Where's the ring, darling?"
>
> "I'll make one. Here is the ring. You mustn't laugh, Gee, or St. Michael will be cross and say we must come again another day. Now we cross the Ford. Then for the bank of violets–it will be all dark-green in this light, and the waterfall will be thundering like an organ.". . .
>
> They were children of the moor, and they were to be joined together like earth and sun in the invisible bonds and splendid warmth of a passionately chaste love. (476-477)

The overtones here are like that of the old pagan *Pervigilium Veneris*–the springtime awakening of plants and animals under the aegis of Venus, life-giving "procreatrix"–and suggest a dialogue between sun and earth, male and female, in which love becomes the symbol of a hidden meaning beyond the abyss.Although the journey of life has a dark heart of loneliness, George and Winnie recognize in their life-threatening disease and its anxiety of biological extinction a battle between divine and demonic forces; they then forge an unbreakable existence in each other.

At the story's end, the ever-sane Gregory Breakback still longs for female companionship–"the only solution of the great problem of the lonely void of space which the gods allow men" (5). If the wind is seen by George as purity that heals the body (408), Gregory likewise credits it as that which brought him "along" (458). Gregory proposes to Ada even though she had laughed at his vision of the wind. But when Ada discloses the indiscretions of her youth, Gregory couldn't "break and bend his back" (460). (Despite the pun that suggests a characternym, Trevena takes pains to point out that this and related odd names are historic in the area, not merely fantastic.) A stiff growth with his iron rod and sheep-dog, Gregory cannot reach through the temporal loneliness of his existence; death will be "necessary to make the dream real" (461). The failure and the triumph of Gregory's death looks forward to old Will Yeo and his son Mark in the next novel: "it was not sad, for tragedy makes a man sublime" (*Granite,* 436).

Granite

On the copyright page of *Granite* and in a cocky advertisement in the *Devon and Exeter Gazette*, Alston Rivers announced this novel as "Published, October 27. Reprinted, October 28." Also in this same publisher's advertisement a reviewer is quoted as saying: "the time of mere promise has clearly passed. 'Granite' is a far finer, far more mature book than 'Furze' or 'Heather.'" But one wonders how pleased its author may have been to read that "it raises Mr. Trevena to the level of Mr. Phillpotts, far above the rank and file of English genre novelists" ("Publisher's Advertisement" 10). A more percipient reviewer of the concluding volume of this "great moorland trilogy" placed its author–admittedly in rather generalized phrases–"in the very first rank of modern writers of fiction. Indeed, in his own field as a student of purely country life and character, we know of no writer of the present day–Thomas Hardy having abandoned fiction–who can at all compare with him for insight, true knowledge of nature, power of vigorous writing" ("Publisher's Notice," *Westminster Gazette* [ii]). The *Boston Evening Transcript* added: "Nothing in 'Granite' makes for hurried reading. Like its predecessors, it is written for the deep thought of many a leisure hour and for that sort of intellectual pleasure that absorbs itself in the innermost recesses of human evil and human good. It is a story of Dartmoor, but it is at the same time a story of the world at large" (Rev. of *Granite* 18). Set further east in Dartmoor with probably Chagford as the original of "Fursdon," *Granite* opens with an allegory of its eponymousstone, a mineral that encapsulates evolutionary stages and emblematizes mankind's (and womankind's–terms here are not gender specific) difficult history. Perhaps this explains why here for once Trevena gives a more-detailed account than usual of the tools and particular activities of the local workmen's labor. Job's father's wall with cruel brambles growing out of it encloses a fir garden. At sunset, a man who "stands beside the wall while the sun is bleeding among the brambles" is himself scratched. With its "sword of heat and sandals of light" the caged Promethean sun longs to free man who is "tortured by vultures of passion and disease"(*Granite* 2). Man with his mattock wants to help the bleeding sun escape from the snagging brambles, but to make a wall out of the granite of human misery, its passion and disease, is simply to give brambles a place to grow.

An amused wee voice of a "zoophyte," half-plant half-animal trapped in a stone of the wall, expresses mankind's inner awareness, "the funny little voice of consciousness" telling a gnomic parable (7): slow progress is the order of the universe; man is not creation's greatest wonder, merely a descendant of the zoophyte; the true wonder is creation's beginning; this is the only miracle except for those in myths. The previous two novels of the trilogy had been introduced by similar voices from the past–mythic, historical, and now here fantastic. The wall has many rocks, mankind has many parts–genius, cruelty, strength–that make up his living whole. Because of any human's infinitesimal place in nature, the actual accomplishment of wall building is trifling–the earth belongs to the brambles and furze; nature is man's master, "the rock that his mind splits upon"(8). Sun, zoophyte, man–all are caged by the wall-like recalcitrance of facticity. Splitting the granite and building a wall of the pieces is, certainly in one lifetime, futile–one cannot improve the all but unimproveable in a day, nor in a lifetime, nor in a geological era. Walls (whether things or theories, dogs or dogmas) keep elements apart and harden them into non-entity and death.

A strong current of nineteenth-century philosophical Idealism recognized that such emotional or ideological entrapment–as symbolized by cages, walls, tombs or ticking clocks–means that transcendental truth cannot be disclosed directly, only glimpsed in symbols that turn the broken and the estranged back upon themselves, transforming dying moment into dying moment by regeneration through destruction, linking mortality to some higher but far off source of renewal within the external relationships of the whole. It is easy to imagine the young Henham returning from the Continent with Henri Bergson's recently published *L'Évolution créatrice* (1907), pondering on that "vital impetus" behind the evolution of living things that Bergson identified so convincingly with consciousness. Mankind's walls are certainly *within* some "sustained, forward-pushing vitality of orderly intelligible relationships" suggested in antiquity by Heraclitus (*The Fragments* 45-47) and also by Trevena's up-to-date culture; but only if taken collectively are they *of* those "ordinances of the divine reason, maintained throughout the changes of the phenomenal world" (Pater, *Marius* 1:141). Human systems, like circumscribing walls, are always limited by the places and times that created them, are already part of the future's past; and the zoophyte reminds his listener that he also will belong to that past. Nor can that wee primordial voice articulate how, plunging into non-being beyond the "allotted span," one may find "something to hold by and rest on, amid the perpetual flux" (1:166-167).The zoophyte's seemingly rather trite moral (it *is* just a talking zoophyte after all) is that the greatest thing in man is the strength that triumphs over his weakness. But this can be fattened up a bit if one connects strength-over-weakness to that which in the previous novel had been the heather's endurance in the tearing wind; and if one then connects that to those who in their self-affirmation participate in the historical selfconsciousness of mankind. This historic order of human though in its mutation and opposition becomes that "harmony" or "principle of sanity and reality in things" (1:141).

Trevena's favorite blue flower, the saxifrage, makes use of the crevices in the place of brambles to symbolizethis healing of the radical estrangement within the human condition, a bridging and a drawing of life forward toward "the holy" beyond the *flamentia moenia mundi*. Thus the saxifrage, which Trevena says does not split the rocks in which it grows, seizes upon preexisting fissures–those violent fractures–to turn them to account in its flowering beauty by which the cleavage is healed. Hence imaginative vision is less a sentimental cliché than a powerfully transforming tool of cognition:

> It was the beautiful vision which makes men and women feel unexpectedly and so briefly, that life is excellent, the deed is possible, good is easy; gives them the quick, joyous flush of faith, lends them greatness. This thrill, which is everything but real, comes to everyone, especially to those who would love well and to those who would think well. It is false, because it reveals too much, and neither lover nor thinker can reach high enough. Each sees and feels, then hurries off from the fountains in the rock, from the bed of white flowers in the moonlight, but, with the mistress in his arms, or the pen between his fingers, what is he but a man again? The divinity has trickled out of his clay. The fruit remains upon the top of the tree. And yet, it shows there must be a soul-world somewhere, for the mind has felt it. (*Granite* 288)

Because the Romantics' symbols blend the eternal with the temporal, the infinite with the finite, they enable the self to see the temporal-historical world as no longer foreign but as that in which its own higher collective identity consists.

One could observe that *Granite* is a novel with at least two threads of plot conflict. One reviewer found it "the struggles of two men of widely differing birth, education, and character to become worthy of a woman" ("News of Books" BR352); and another found its central conflict between Squire Vivian–who wants to keep the status quo by tolerating drunkenness, idleness, and debauchery–and Mark Yeo, the stone-breaker's son and temperance revivalist. Mark is the common figure in both these plot conflicts. Self-educated and a colonially-ordained preacher, Mark pits his frail strength against the Squire's culture of established customs, waging wrathful war on drunkenness in his native village of Fursdon. Squire Vivian is a "colonial" character who may well be based on historical figures from within Dartmoor. Among such actual figures, Thomas Tyrwhitt is an excellent example of the squirearchy–

> calling at the start of the nineteenth century for the colonisation of Dartmoor on a parallel with Canada. . . . Their social life was divorced from the people they lived among; their friends came on long-distance visits using the new roads and railways; their wives enjoyed the seasons in London and in fashionable gathering places such as Bath; their sons and daughters married the sons and daughters of other squires and clergy all over the country. To them Devon was landscape, and the detachment from the everyday concerns of local people that such a view of the area produced made it an ideal hunting ground for the amateur naturalist and antiquary. This was reflected in the legacy handed down to twentieth-century Devon fiction. (Beeson 175)

In *Granite,* Squire Vivian amused himself with the abuse of his position. He "could not restrain his power nor yet his love for conjuring with souls, tossing them up and down to see how they acted, and if any fell and were damaged it was all in the game. . . . His mind despised and hated his fellow-creatures while his tongue declared it liked them" (314).

As Trevena observed in *Furze*, "Drunkenness is not a vice upon Dartmoor; nor a fault even. It is a custom" (80). And he sees this "custom" in particular as the cause of the ill-treatment of women who age quickly: Mary Tavy, Barseba Starke, Ursula Petherick, or Thirza Billacott "who toiled in a shameful skirt, boots made for a ploughman, a ragged cloth cap, a sack around her shoulders"(*Sleeping Waters*74). In childhood, Mark had seen a frightening shadow on the granite, a sign that guided him: "He was so far different from other young men of his class that he could perceive these shadows; not by his own learning, but through the power of observation given him by the thing, the cloudy sign, the shadow upon granite, which was not there really but was in himself and was as inexplicable as is the whole nature of man" (*Granite* 17). This sign, emanating from himself, seemed alternately to threaten or to promise and it progressively strengthens until near the end of the story it begins to disappear and finally, as Mark says, "the river had washed it away" (139-140, 362, 446-447). When he called out rhetorically, "Why has it forsaken me?" (446)–an echo surely of Psalm 22:1 and the words from the Cross–did Trevena intend to suggest a spiritual crisis of unbearable and inescapable loneliness for Mark centering on the weight of others' guilt? Or on the barriers that separate him from Edith? Or on doubts about the correctness and success of his calling? Certainly a loneliness that cannot be filled is slowly eroding his effectiveness. Trevena most likely is using the same Nordic idea he employed in *Tenebrae*: the self is both a human body and an enveloping spirit strong enough to take visible form and follow its physical twin like a shadow–and if seen is often a portent of approaching death.

The father of Mark is Will Yeo, the life-long clearer of rocks from a worthless field and builder of walls, who has worked with the boulders until he resembled one himself:

> Old Will looked like one of those fantastic figures which centuries of hard weather have chiselled out of the black rocks of the tors. He was so massive and dark with scars, and his old clothes clung to him like moss and lichen; the dust of granite had become engrained in his skin: his beard was full of it, and flakes of mica glittered upon his arms, and his teeth were like quartz-splinters, his face was red with iron-ore, and his boots were green with copper. (*Granite* 233)

For sixty-five Sisyphean years Will pitted his strength against these adamantine obstacles of the fields. Sisyphus defied the gods, putting Death in chains so that no humans should die, but the gods freed Death and punished Sisyphus himself. He was condemned to push a rock ceaselessly and pointlessly up a mountain; at the top the rock would roll down leaving Sisyphus to begin the act anew–a metaphor in Albert Camus's essay, "The Myth of Sisyphus" (1942), for the inescapable meaninglessness of modern life. Sisyphus's punishment is an analogue for Will's never-ending splitting of granite that, in Trevena's version, is owing to always yet more stubborn rocks and to man's infinitesimal duration in comparison with geological time.

But if for old Will as for Sisyphus the "granite" of the world remains unconquered, neither hero is defeated. The tragic moment in Sisyphus's toil is to see the boulder roll down again; but when he accepts the futility of his task, he is freed to realize his situation and to reach heroic self-affirmation. Camus' last line is: "The struggle itself is enough to fill a man's heart. One must imagine Sisyphus happy" (*Camus* 123). Mark's battle against drunkenness, preaching vainly in the face of the commoners' indifference and ignorance, basically leaves the region and its vices unchanged: "he and his father would die, the granite and the evil would still be left unconquered" (*Granite* 233). The Yeos's stubbornness is like Sisyphus's heroic acceptance. Indeed, Trevena's commentary on old Will's dying seems an anticipation of Camus' conclusion: "The father had finished his fight, the son was entering the last phase of his, but it was not sad, for tragedy makes a man sublime. And life is a tragedy because death comes to it; and all life is sublime because it ends; heroism is forced upon it. . . ." (436) and the remainder of this paragraph is equally splendid. But Trevena's belief in "a soul-world somewhere" is an element not in Camus' philosophy of the Absurd, so the Sisyphean assault by Will and Mark on the "granite" of Dartmoor perforce carries a somewhat altered meaning, not unlike nuances of difference between the import of Tregeagle's punishment (*Pixy* 157) and that of Sisyphus. Mankind's master is nature, and its walls, like the material reality of granite, brambles, and furze, represent the givenness of reality. All man's explanations of Truth become lower-cased truths, rock-like ideological entities upon which "his mind splits." But the mystery of the temporal manifold in which humans exist is that somehow it both is and is not present within the *totum simul*–the mystery of the Ineffable within every human moment.Like the monitory utterances of Socrates's "dæmon," old Will hears voices among the rocks, something like the clairvoyance of divine interventions it may be.

The other narrative line in *Granite*, its sub-plot if you will,centers on Gerard Spiller, a young curate hired by his croquet-playing rector to attend to parish duties,and again on Mark, mystic and reformer. Both men are of humble birth and frail physical strength, yet by education are of dissimilar professional classes andmarkedly unalike in strength of character. They are rivals for the hand of the upper-class Edith Gribbin, who is not entirely plain in her appearance but emphatically puritanical in her practice. Edith, says Trevena, "uplifted the soul and did not enkindle the body" (201-202). The Squire, as a sort of Lord Henry Wotton figure, has led Gerard into an alcoholism from which he cannot find the strength "to triumph over his own weakness" (6). Trevena seems very much influenced by the stance of the Temperance Movement against the consumption of alcoholic drinks and by those Catholic and Nonconformist clergymen who saw the disastrous effects of drunkenness upon husbands and wives, parents and children, and called for improvement in the deplorable living conditions that drove the poor to drink. Edith had begun to carve on a beech tree a symbolic square of love, parallel lines that were to be joined to two more, marking her unwavering foursquare determination to accept only a man free of alcohol. Gerard meanwhile has conformed himself and his career to the prevailing social mores, avoiding exposure to controversy by rejecting the challenge of reform and accepting with complacency the life-style choices of Squire, Rector, and locals. As Gerard betrays Edith's trust by lying about abstaining from strong drink, she discovers that her tree has been cut down and debranched, a "dismembered giant" destined for the saw-mill (480). She brands Gerard a "liar," an appropriate final epithet, Trevena comments, for "a work dealing with human nature" (482). Although Gerard loses Edith as he slips toward disintegration, she is not sufficiently flexible or visionary to understand Mark's half-mad genius; so the possibility of that mutual relationship also perishes.

Among the other supporting cast of characters is Edith's guardian Mrs. Allen, a self-regarding figure of the gentry who uses cocaine, subjects Edith to stupid cruelties, faces a shoplifting charge, and plans to poison Edith to keep her from testifying–in short, self-centered to the point of criminality. Then there is the commoner George Vid who, like Pendoggat in *Furze*, cruelly cheats the half-witted and deluded Coales, a Brightly figure. Trevena also devotes several full chapters to the "child-brothers" (270) Eli and Oli and their cats, Tom and his prolific female companion, Ted. The brothers' role is to be the narrative's standard of naive innocence, the even beat of their lives measured by "grandfather" who is only interrupted when a shyster clock repairman from the outer world disturbs his inner workings. Their potential for either financial cunning or mystical vision is naively latent in the brothers, just as a moral sexual conscience is simply not part of Ted's reproductive awareness. More central as figures are the two sisters Temperance and Patience Starke, who derive their names from 2 Peter 1:5-8: "Add to your faith . . . knowledge; and to knowledge temperance; and to temperance patience; and to patience godliness...." Their names are typical of Non-conformist denominations, but since it is Temperance who has both qualities and Patience who has neither, the ironies of human nature and piety are deepened. Patience, the prostitute whom Mark works to save–if not with devotion and sacrifice, then with the terror of exposure for her crimes–grew up with her sister Tempy at Love Lane Farm where the boulders struck out as though escaping from "the deep womb of the earth" (332). Her ingrained sensuality is another form of the rocky farmyard: "That ground would not respond to gentle treatment; it had to be fought with hammers and dynamite and its answer was a curse" (20). Rounding out the cast is Barsaba's stag-turkey, a stronger animal personality even than Mary's goose Old Sal. Like Sal who is "cruel human" (*Furze*9), the turkey shares the novel's motif of iron self-discipline. He is "a sort of bishop among the birds," celibate and hating females, and he tolerated men "with cynicism because they were weak where he was strong" (*Granite* 24). Eventually he hid himself in the farmyard and starved to death like an old stoic (335). Along with this steadfast turkey, Mark and old Will come to similarly stubborn ends–old Will among his boulders, Mark worn out and disillusioned.

In his efforts to refashion fallen human nature, Mark compulsively dualizes drunkenness and temperance. But the antithesis of the demonic to the divine is not fixed, like some Manichaean division of matter and spirit; rather, it is a dialogue that enables each to appear as if it were the vehicle of the other's tenor–unfathomable, surdal, and incommensurable contraries perpetually turning back, the one upon the other. Mark discounts entirely this ineradicable rootedness of opposites that nest one within the other, and that is why the voices in the wind and the shadows on the rocks' surfaces suggest to him an "uncomfortable mystery" (98)–that the universe is built upon or exists through this play of contraries, each understood in terms of its opposite as darkness is through light. Hence for Trevena the precondition to any human joy, like the necessity of enduring winter's spell of sterility to attain spring's new life, is a recognition that the possibilities of deliverance must always be darkened at their sources by the fragmentation of the diabolic that precedes it. This is why in *Heather* George and Winnie, who courageously love both because of and in the face of their incurable illnesses, still find joy. Mark's labor, like that of his father, is a heroism that emerges as Sisyphean because it has not encompassed or adjusted to the possibility of this fundamental *je ne sais quoi* . . . should one call it a “mirism” or a “paradoxical paradigm”?

CHAPTER 8

BRACKEN (1910) | *WINTERING HAY* (1912)

Bracken

Arnold Bennett protested when the Censorship Committee of the United Circulating Libraries put "its ban absolute upon Mr. John Trevena's new novel 'Bracken.' It is true that quite a number of people had considered Mr. Trevena to be a serious and dignified artist of rather considerable talent. . . . The Censorship Committee must justify its existence somehow. Mr. Trevena ought to have dedicated his wretched provincial novel to the Queen of Montenegro. He painfully lacks *savoir-vivre*" (*Books and Persons* 276). Bennett's caustic commentary exposes both the Committee's own provincialism and its readiness to censor an easy target. But other reviewers could have put the Committee's alleged minds at rest: "it is almost unreadable" said the *Saturday Review* (Rev. of *Bracken* 87); F.T. Cooper concurred: "it fails to be intelligible" (339). Whereas *Furze* had seemed closer to Trevena's realistic vein, though with elements of Devonshire superstitions mixed throughout, *Bracken* foregrounds Trevena's mystic tendencies, that confounding part of our nature in which, as the existentialist Simone de Beauvoir once said, "things of the spirit come first" (her book's title). *Bracken*, wrote one approving reviewer, "tells of people prehistoric and magical":

> The story takes us into a world drowned, as it were, in a mysterious ocean, an atmosphere that magnifies and distorts. The men and women are of our own day and customs, to be sure, but they seem different, almost prehistoric, linked to the beginnings of things, framed with magic. It is the deep, black roots of us that Mr. Trevena digs up and exposes to the light–roots that unite us with the ancient mother and whose dark flowers we have smothered out of sight in the long processes of civilization.

> It is the story of a human soul in its triumph and failure, its good and evil, its all-besetting pride; and the story of the fall of Lucifer, in fact, in modern dress. . . . Mr. Trevena tells his story with a certain aloof poetry both in the conception and the execution. Though it has to do with much that is dark and hideous, it remains beautiful. A sense of awe is conveyed of the working of great forces, and though the end is darkness, there are hints of ultimate light, and a little sound of love and laughter from two simple creatures who have found happiness for themselves in mutual understanding and devotion. ("Mystic's Tale" BR163)

Plot is subordinate to character and character is subordinate to theme.

A slightly later overview in *Current Opinion* re-introduced the by-now established contrast with Phillpotts to deplore exactly that which made Trevena the superior writer:

> Trevena's work has been often compared to that of Eden Phillpotts. An eye and a tongue for the grandeur and beauty of a natural scene in which human figures have their place, a sort of Olympian humor, an appreciation of the littleness and dearness and fundamental wholesomeness of man are qualities *The Nation* discovers in both writers. But *The Nation* does not find the healthy optimism of Phillpotts in the novels of John Trevena.
>
> "Even at the outset he wandered perilously near the line that divides what is grim from what is morbid. His realism lacked the balance-wheel of health which has protected the realism of Mr. Phillpotts in the most desperate conditions. Often a young author (Trevena is not very young, but his authorship may still be called so) grows into such health. This one appears to have lost all chance of it. The confused fanciful melancholy of 'Bracken,' its misdirected or undirected ardor of imagination, its moral impotence, are to be found again, if less repellently, in 'Wintering Hay.'" (429)

But one must not approach *Bracken* with the expectation of self-explanatory "healthy optimism." More helpfully, Elia Peattie found Trevena "a psychologist who feels both a scientific and a spiritual interest in the processes of man's mind, and who is asking terrible questions concerning the power of the mind of one man over another. Evidently a student of morbid psychology, he has read whatever has been written upon multiple personality, the transference of characteristics, and telepathic influence, and he has supplemented these amazing facts with all that his abundant and gloomy imagination can provide" ("Among the New Books" 11).

Although this was an era of arrogant scientific confidence in which Lord Kelvin was quoted as saying that "the grand underlying principles" of physical reality "have been firmly established" and all that remains is "determining values to a greater number of decimal places" (Greene 9), Trevena preferred another school of science: the respected Society for Psychical Research, co-founded by Henry Sedgwick and Frederic Myers at Trinity College, Cambridge, to investigate hypnotic, psychic, and spiritualistic events. A report of a ghost encountered by Henham/Trevena appeared as case "G 274 'Apparition'" in the 1903-1904 Society *Journal* describing his encounter with a well-known deceased woman in 1899 while bicycling through Oxford. (This was, of course, the era of the bicycle "revolution" which brought liberation to the congested city-dweller and speed and freedom to the villages.) He relates that:

> There was no possible doubt about the identity–if I may so use the word in this connection. I have such a strong memory that if I only pass a person on the street, I remember the face if I see it again. Besides, Miss S., once seen, could never be mistaken for any one else. . . . I may mention that I have rather peculiar eyesight, more powerful I suppose than is ordinary, because it enables me to see in the dark. . . . Fortunately my aunt keeps a diary, and often puts down my little expeditions, and it was from her diary that I discovered the day was November 15, and as I remember reaching my destination (Summertown) about 3:15, it must roughly have been 3 when I saw Miss S. However, I can prove the date in another way. It is a wearisome journey from here to Oxford by train, and though I have often been to Oxford I have *always* bicycled. I came to live here in July, 1899, and being a horseman I had then a hatred for bicycles. But after a time I saw that to a dweller in the country a machine was indispensable, and being unable to keep a horse I resolved on getting a bicycle. . . .

He bought his bike in Reading two or three days before the death of Miss S. on the 5th or 6th of October and still has his receipt dated

3 October; he even adds that he "did not begin to learn to ride until several days after" his purchase (Trevena, *Short Stories* 5-7).

A valuable but succinct review of *Bracken* recognizes Trevena's indebtedness to such events as were reported and probed by the Society: "Unlike 'Furze the Cruel,' 'Heather,' and 'Granite,' this new novel, although using the moorland symbolism, has not a word of Devonshire dialect, nor are there any rustics among its characters. It deals with the influence of a morbid mind upon that of a weak neurotic woman, which destroys the original mind altogether. Later, the influence of a healthy mind brings out a third type, which is permanent. It is said that the leading idea of the story was suggested by a case quoted in Frederick Myers's 'Human Personality'" ("American History" BR44). Frederic (no "k" in his given name) W.H. Myers (1843–1901), a forerunner of modern psychic research, published *Human Personality and its Survival of Bodily Death* in 1903. He scrupulously investigated both the self-aware and subconscious minds, hoping to render "the satisfaction of scientific curiosity as to man's psychical structure" (1:68) and to argue successfully for life beyond "bodily death." If Trevena's *Bracken* is not the first novel to deal with the multiple personalities of a single character, it is surely among the first to draw upon an actual psychological case history with such conscious deliberation. One thinks, of course, of R.L. Stevenson's *Dr. Jekyll and Mr. Hyde* (1885); however, that was a theologically Calvinist allegory; *Bracken*, on the other hand, stays within scientific factuality as then documented.

Frederic Myers reported the case of "the Misses Beauchamp," a college student who was treated at first as "a neurasthenic of a very severe type" and "a wreck, I might say, in body" (neurasthenia is an obsolete term for chronic fatigue, lack of motivation, and overwhelming feelings of inadequacy). Miss Beauchamp, as described by her analyst and quoted in Myers, "is a very serious-minded person, fond of books and study, of a religious turn of mind, and possesses a very morbid conscientiousness. She has a great sense of responsibility in life." But when hypnotized and in a "somnambulistic state," two other "distinct and separate" personalities spontaneously emerge. This patient corresponds to Trevena's Margaret. When Margaret "began to rub her eyes and to cry, 'I want to wake up. I have been asleep all my life'" (*Bracken* 54), her actions and words are exactly what Miss Beauchamp does and says when hypnotized in her analyst's office. And thereupon the "Sally" Beauchamp personality, who is Trevena's Lucy, replaces the original Miss Beauchamp:

> Sally, on the other hand, is full of fun, does not worry about anything; all life is one great joke to her, she hates books, loves fun and amusement, does not like serious things, hates church, in fact is thoroughly childlike in every way. She is a child of nature. She is not as well educated as is Miss Beauchamp. . . . She is never fatigued. . . . Though Miss Beauchamp knows nothing of Sally, Sally, when not in the flesh, is conscious of all Miss Beauchamp's thoughts and doings, and the latter could hide nothing from her. Curiously enough, Sally took an intense dislike to [her] . . . She actually hated her . . . and there was no length to which Sally would not go to cause her annoyance. (Meyers 1:344-345)

And the "third personality," who is a very different character from either the original Miss Beauchamp or "Sally" Beauchamp becomes Trevena's "Mary." This third Miss Beauchamp displays a "formal and distant attitude":

> Unlike the others, she is irritable and quick-tempered, and resented as an impertinence–especially as she regarded most of us as strangers–any inquiry into her private thoughts and affairs, and above all any interference with her habits of life and private conduct. Though anxious to know, she was not willing to ask about what had occurred in the gaps when the others were in the flesh, and so was in the habit of inferring and guessing, at which she was very skillful. . . . But [she] is more than a match for Sally, who is really afraid of her. They quarrel like cats and dogs. (1:346-350)

Myers reports these personalities as developments of Miss Beauchamp's "subliminal consciousness, which . . . has obtained finally an independent existence, and led an individual life of its own"; but he also cites evidence that allows Trevena to give to the Misses Beauchamp what Myers designates as "a communication between the minds of [different] living persons, independently of the action of the recognised organs of sense":

> We may still call this a *telepathic impact*, if we will, but we shall find it hard to distinguish that term from a *psychical invasion*, . . . –an invasion no longer of the room only in which the percipient is sitting, but of his own body and his own powers. It is an invasion which, if sufficiently prolonged, would become a *possession*. . . . What seemed at first a mere impact is tending to become a persistent control; what seemed an incursion merely into the percipient's environment has become an incursion into his organism itself. (2:82-83, 186)

What Trevena did with Myers's case history of Miss Beauchamp is what every writer would do–he upped the ante on the facts as reported about this specific case, not so much as to stretch credibility or as would call into play the reader's "willing suspension of disbelief," but sufficient for a frisson of chill down the spine: the "intercalary occupation by an external spirit" in Myers's scholarly terminology (2:192). And clearly, these additional factors would be entirely believable inasmuch as this was the era of Rasputin's reported ascendancy over the Tsar and Tsarina of Russia.

Although the topography and flora of *Bracken* indeed do belong loosely to Dartmoor (43, 371), unlike in Trevena's previous novels the strongly regional setting has now become a more psychically inner locale. However, the personification of natural forces and a mystical aura annex *Bracken* thematically to the trilogy of furze, heather, and granite. But each of the other trilogy narratives, unlike *Bracken*, opens with a fantasy speaker contrasting past and present, invoking the lineal span of epochs that impact each other. But in all four novels there is a correspondence between man and the life forces of nature that mold the predominant traits of the dwellers on the Moor. Beyond the three ground covers of furze, heather, and granite lies a cover of fern that elevates the previously treated life-traits of working-day cruelty, endurance, and strength into the hidden world within and without phenomenal reality. The bracken and its roots, sole surviving plants of the Paleozoic or "carboniferous" era, represent the primordial world of the life-force that persists in the depths of human consciousness: "the root is our destiny, the seed our future; in the blossoms we see ourselves as we would be" (214). The trees rotting among the bracken are like decaying bodies: "To walk through those fields was to hear sermons. The rough path suggested the way of life; first the vicious furze, then the heather clinging to the open space, and the unyielding boulders leaning in the next, and the mysterious fern sleeping in the last. The path went through these to end in rottenness and decay deep down beyond" (27-28).

Bracken is a mystic's tale of a superannuated but robust teacher, Ramrige the wise "master"; of his erstwhile sullen pupil, Cuthbert Orton, a genius of libidinous proclivities; and of a sweetly dreamy but impressionable young lady, Margaret Rose Vipont, who is first ensnared by Cuthbert's books and then after a personal but platonic encounter is seduced. Margaret lives with her father, an antiques dealer, and with his sister under thatch at Cob Court, an ancient residence not far from Cuthbert's more stylish abode. As the plot commences, Jasper grows aware that the schoolboy Cuthbert is thrusting himself into his personal psyche and their two lives begin to twist together like strands in a rope. Cuthbert reproaches his schoolmaster for decapitating with his stick the ferns that ooze and die like living things and says he is "murdering mysteries" (6). Frederic Myers had observed that "we come to regard consciousness as an attribute which may possibly be present in all kinds of varying degrees in connection with the animal and vegetable world; as the psychical counterpart of life; as conceivably the psychical counterpart of all phenomenal existence" (Meyers 1:37). Cuthbert and Jasper become less friends than philosophical adversaries, personalities tied telepathically through Margaret by the bracken's roots: Jasper is the oak, Margaret the fern, Cuthbert the bog and its "decay deep down beyond" (*Bracken* 28, 255-256, 265-266).

Like Margaret, both master and pupil also long to find "that idealism of a perfect self" (62) and were led by "the natural unreasoning impulse which guides animals, that mystic flash of clear intelligence, whatever other name it may be called, which causes even the lowest grub to imitate exactly the parents it has no knowledge of" (9). This instinct seems to have arranged monitory encounters between Jasper and Cuthbert; yet at first neither could understand, for "one mind was dumb, the other was deaf, and both were ignorant" (30). Although these figures cannot access what the poet Hopkins called "inscape" and "instress," that divine and unique pattern and energy in nature, Trevena has Cuthbert pondering this pattern in a leaf, how "to the eye of nature that leaf was possibly unlike all others, endowed with a personality of its own by some deep principle of life which had marked its surface with peculiar veins, jagged its edges with a form unlike others, given it a certain texture or shade of colour not found elsewhere" (25). Cuthbert's tragedy is that if "the world is charged with the grandeur of God" (Hopkins), he cannot access this "instress" or divine energy. Nature is a wholly veiled Isis: "She can come to me with flower for face, and mosses for feet, and garments made of fern-fronds, or she may send a dream for kindliness, one cold star for a sign, a flash of spiritual insight to keep me sane, but she is not with me. She remains at an eternity's distance, while she is around, behind, above" (23).

Several allusions hint at something more than a semi-autobiographical significance in the novel. Cuthbert is born exactly on Trevena's birthday (16) and Cuthbert's fiancée Ethel dies, owing, it is hinted, to his mainly selfish love. Henham/Trevena too had lost a fiancée and afterwards wandered the Moor talking to this deceased beloved. Another allusion to Trevena's life springs from the very center of Dartmoor's nested boxes: Duchy of Cornwall, Rockside, Summerland Village, Cob Court, and "wrapped in white like cotton-wool the treasure upon a bed: not a withered flower but a Rose in bloom, not an old pearl but a Margaret glowing" (46). Marguerite is French for "daisy," derived from the Greek "margarite" that means "pearl"; Rose was the middle name of Trevena's wife-to-be by which everyone knew her. Trevena may be reaching here toward an identification of himself with Cuthbert, the pupil turned master, and of his wife Rose with the multiplex personality of Margaret, appropriately introduced with a metaphor of nested boxes.Like Cuthbert, Trevena himself was said "to be a source of some terror to the nearest village, as the superstitious people regarded him as a magician." Margaret Rose's surname of Vipont (originally, at the time of William the Conqueror, spelled as Vieuxpont: "old bridge") was the name adopted by her father from a long-dead bishop; perhaps Trevena was thinking of her bridging between the innocence of the white Rose and the passion of the red. She may be understood to have inherited her unstable personality from this epileptic father, inasmuch as Myers relates such seizures to her multiple personality disorder (1:339). Perhaps Trevena's own Rose was a "woman who sees visions" and, like

Margaret "the mystical fern-woman," was "troubled by the winds underneath the arms of her oak-husband" (*Bracken* 256). Trevena's image of "the oak tree in the stem of the bracken," one may recall, has migrated from *Heather* (174). The reader may speculate that Trevena by endowing Cuthbert and Margaret with aspects of his actual life is deliberately experimenting with alternative personalities, perhaps by mixing hypothetical details with personal facts to examine covertly the depths of his own personality.

Margaret is one in whom imagination dwells but her problem is emotional neediness. Her "musical dreams" (*Bracken* 90) express a delight that carries one, as Myers says, "through an ideal and unimaginable world. . . . Music resembles not so much a product of terrene needs and of natural selection as a subliminal capacity attaining to . . . the supraliminal self" (Myers 1:101, 103). Genius is defined by Myers as "the co-operation of the submerged with the emergent self–as the integration of the subliminal with the supraliminal faculty" (1:96). Margaret's transcription of the songs that she believes to be the sounds of nature recalls Mark Yeo's projection of himself in the sign on the rocks, both emanate from within: "She would have heard them had she been stone deaf" (*Bracken* 61-62). And similarly, Cuthbert's more sinister projections create victims yet recoil upon himself. He has experimented with his ability to dominate women–the headmaster's daughter, perhaps his fiancée, and later a promiscuous woman of mixed race. Afterwards Margaret yields to his poisonous influence until, by his mental desires or, as Peattie says, by a "direct emanation of all that is most rebellious and hateful in his own nature" (11), he creates Lucy within her. Peattie reads this as a modern version of *Faustus* in which Faust and Mephistopheles become one. But another reviewer found it possible to read here a story of Satan's fall "in modern dress, and clothed in three personalities–a woman, a weak, sweet creature, whose father is an epileptic, and two men, master and pupil" ("Mystic's Tale" BR163). It may be better still to find in Lucy's name, like that of Lucifer, a parable of an angel of light–the fallen light bearer, creator of mankind's original sin (2 Corinthians 11:14). Although decades older than Margaret and very much a Walter Pater figure–"of women he knew too little: his own sex was enough: the academic life and the beauty of boys made up his world" (*Bracken* 7)–Jasper finds he loves her and tries daringly to counteract Cuthbert's dominance with his own mental influence, battling him to free her of sensuality and produce a saintly woman of the intellect. But Lucy has become pregnant by Cuthbert and a monstrous creature is born in Jasper's house, quickly euthanized with Jasper's assent by the young physician. The infant is deformed or sexually ambiguous in contrast to nature's rule and purpose; the doctor thus acts to reinstate a quarantine barrier or wall of morality between the parents' unnatural lust and his ideal of a genteel propriety that must govern everything.

Margaret yearningly responds to Jasper's strong and fatherly overtures; as he reads to her the matrimonial service one evening by his fire, "her own self was being consumed, her mind was being purged; and out of those white ashes she would rise again, rebaptized to beauty, married to strength, dead to evil thoughts, the victim of the sacrifice and the goddess to whom it was offered" (271). But when "Mary" emerges afterwards she is no new Phoenix but a coldly rational, unloving, thinking machine desiring only revenge upon Cuthbert, which she calls justice, for her ruined life. It would not be amiss to say that both Cuthbert and Jasper have played Frankenstein, and the creatures that emerge, Lucy and Mary, are the uncontrolled products of flaws within their creators. Jasper's failure was to turn for spiritual answers to astrology (106) rather than to the metetherial beauty within this material world (267); conversely, Cuthbert's flaw was his enslavement by a purely sensual desire although he thought of himself as a man of mind. Still, Cuthbert may be no worse than Jasper. No one in Trevena's fiction who is kind to an animal can be all bad, and Cuthbert's love for his blind dog, as well as his expressed desire to reform, momentarily holds the door open on forgiveness. Jasper and Cuthbert, each in his own way, proudly tries to lead an almost wholly self-sufficient life, projecting his own soul upon the world. In "By Violence" Trevena observes that it is "through the agency of others, through the eyes of those who are loved and loving, not by the confinement of self, souls find the dawn" (*Written . . . Rain* 18). After the death of his fiancéeEthel, Cuthbert, who becomes the high-priest in a cult of himself, tries to find pity and mercy in mother nature, "plunging into the bushes and large ferns to find her, and catching in his hands a toad and snails instead. In earth and space that same mocking silence, and. .

. there was nothing left but madness" (*Bracken* 30). As Trevena says of this too-willing immersion in sheer natural forces: "Nature will ruin a man as surely as any wanton woman if he gives his whole body to her" (373).

At the end, Cuthbert and the multiplex Margaret-become-Lucy-become-Mary are swallowed by a bog on the moor like the brother and sister in Poe's "Fall of the House of Usher." All that is left are two lich flames keeping watch over the primordial forces of nature and the dark subliminal regions of the unconscious mind: "flickering candles were all that remained to earth of two lives; two little unquiet lights, blue and terrible, playing beneath the moon. 'Here are my pupils,' said the master" (406).

Wintering Hay

One object of Trevena's anger in *Wintering Hay* is the deluded, self-righteous religiosity that Edmund Gosse had exposed in *Father and Son* (1903) andthat Samuel Butler had lashed out against in *Ernest Pontifex: The Way of All Flesh* (1903). Trevena's title, which is the name of the farm on which his protagonist lives, denotes winter pasturage that will provide sufficient grasses for animal sustenance. But as the novel's title, it clearly becomes ironic in a psychological sense because Cyril is starved for nourishment. Although the story begins at Christmas there is no spiritual growth or renewal on this land. What Wintering Hay's farm animals perchance represent is neither the miracle of the "ox and ass" in Christina Rossetti's"Bleak Midwinter" nor the encompassing disenchantment in Hardy's "The Oxen." Trevena, on his standpoint between Rossetti's miracle and Hardy's pessimism, pursues in details of ordinary nature an inherent spiritual meaning above or beyond the visible phenomena. He also examines the human conscience and the darker incidents of life, bringing a searching philosophical outlook and achieving an intense psychological insight. The *New York Times* reviewer found his novels:

> Grim stories, most of them, strikingly deficient in what Matthew Arnold phrased as "sweetness and light," but earnest, powerful, sincere, the product of a man who sets down the thing as he sees it, without favor and without fear. . . . There

> are many beautiful descriptions of that Dartmoor which seems to cast a spell over its lovers, that Dartmoor where dwell curious creatures resembling earth gnomes, a place quite unlike any other in the world. A well-wrought novel of an excellent craftsmanship which slurs nothing, a novel which compels belief that the events which it relates really occurred, and occurred for the reasons it assigns, a novel which contains a true and stern picture of the havoc made in other lives by a defect in the character of one not ill-intending man–that is "Wintering Hay." ("Latest Fiction" BR459)

Then an even stronger review in the *Los Angeles Times*–undoubtedly by Paul Jordan-Smith–suggests a penetrating literary comparison:

> Russia has produced the most powerful novelists. Beside Turgenief and Dostoievsky we know of no American and but one Englishman who is fairly entitled to a place. John Trevena alone writes with the force, the dynamic power of the brooding, Slavic titans. However, there is much else than mere power in a great novel; the gift for tragedy does not solely make greatness, and Trevena has more than mere power.
>
> "Wintering Hay" is truly a remarkable book. Yet strong as it is, crushing as it does the lives and hopes of so many of its characters, all the while there seems a reserve force–a conscious effort on the part of the author to hold in restraint his almost tremendous ability to smash and grind the people of his pen. There seems to be no striving for dramatic effects; there is no straining of situations. But there are dramatic effects and tense situations.

Jordan-Smith concludes with a simple, firmly based appraisal of the novel's merits: "There is a touch of mysticism in Mr. Trevena's books; not the opaque, baffling mysticism of professional metaphysicians, but rather the ideals of a dreamer. This quality, combined with his always incisive and sometimes relentless force, and thorough workmanship, enables him to produce novels that are, we believe, to have an honored and permanent classification in literature" ("Powerful Novel" AB 4). Avoiding mere kinetic chaos, his plots are distilled, interpretively, into characterizations by disguised symbols, natural metaphors, subtle gestures, and contextual shadings, almostas if the author were musing on the metaphoric meanings of experiences he himself might have had.

Young Cyril Rossingall, living with his uncle and aunt as had the youthful Ernest Henham, explores on Christmas day a green pixy path with, at its end, a solitary old and dwarfed spruce tree between rocks, configured very much like the crevice-dwelling saxifrages. Such miraculous life in nature did not belong to the outlook of his zealot uncle, Andrew Mutter: "Could he never perceive that the Birth he celebrated was not in ancient history, but present with them, upon every tree in the wood and every primrose in the bank, where every growth was childlike with young buds?" (*Wintering Hay* 8). Trevena's introduction of the novel's characters to the reader is brilliantly handled by means of their responses to Christmas, "the day of all days for wonders" (28): Cyril's belief is in a pagan/Christian God of Nature, his mind steeped in mystical enchantment; Mutter is a puritanical bigot–full of prayers, Scripture readings, and hellfire; Maria, a cottager, is a simple soul longing for upbeat religious hope; Gideon Fley her husband shows a lazy man's totally selfish indifference to all religion; and Kit Coke, Gideon's poacher-friend, finds Christmas an occasion for a cheerful drunk to drink more. Later we will hear of Cyril's good friends George and Lilian Corindon who live on a nearby farm.

That Christmas night, Cyril accidentally kills the drunken Gideon and in fear of consequences persuades Maria, whom Gideon had been threatening and abusing, to help him dispose of the body secretly.They bury him on the moor and Cyril's Christmas tree, planted now above Gideon's grave in "an acre of brambles" (19), becomes the tree of death in the fallen Garden of the world. But in the quaint Renaissance allegorizing of "Hymn to God, My God," John Donne observes "We think that Paradise and Calvary, / Christ's Cross, and Adam's tree, stood in one place." Because the cross was made from wood that grew from the seed of the forbidden tree and its root rested in Adam's grave, moral failure might have become the seed-bed of righteousness. But perversely this initial act of weakness haunts Cyril's life. Trevena dramatizes the angst of a man laboring under a Dostoyevsky-like criminality, a haunting guilt he cannot shake, in which his original sin branches out to still greater tragedies. As in the Slavic imagination, Trevena's atmosphere of guilt andpunishment or of a quiescence only after suffering probes the depths and heights of spiritual metaphysics. He cannot confess the accident to his uncle or to his high-principled girlfriend, Lilian Corindon, and only later does so to her brother George who admires Cyril with a sacrificial devotion. This guilt precipitates other acts of sin such as having "hastened the inevitable death of his kindliest friend" (510), driven a young girl into the slums to have her throat cut, and, bitterly ironic, selfishly makes the devoted George pay a greater price in personal happiness than Cyril himself, for "moral cowardice was bound to lead to acts more fearful than naked unmorality" (509). When Cyril searches for his Christmas pixy path, he finds only dull reality (367). Innocence of heart is needed for the magical vision.

For a time, Cyril finds himself in London's underworld, bu-towing to the sight of his drunken *doppelgänger* and "evil spirit," Adolph Carr, who lies moaning on steps from which he cannot rise, Cyril narrowly escapes a fall into dissipation (286, 292). Later, the gentle mystic and clergyman, Squire Tucker of Broom Hill, reads Cyril's secrets correctly: he knows all about the original manslaughter, a mental penetration of the factual circumstances impossible to explain rationally. Tucker's real life was in the occult world of his deceased wife and daughter with whom he communicates. When Cyril calls him a spiritualist he replies: "You are a spiritualist too. You cannot escape. You are a materialist only when you pamper the body; in your thoughts and dreams you are a spirit" (314). Tucker, the exemplary figure of spirituality, had said once before: "There is no spot in the whole world which is not haunted; no spot where the voices are not heard and the spiritual life is not present" (305). As in *Bracken*, Trevena again advances the suggestion, in connection with Cyril's psyche, of a mental flow of images between minds. Cyril reflects about the Squire: "It did seem that future events were sometimes revealed to him; he did appear to know something about the dead of others; and he did seem able to describe figures and places which Cyril had seen and he had not. Possibly a strong active mind, working unconsciously upon his failing one, transferred its images; as the nearness of the body to its death may have surrounded it with the vision known as spiritual" (350).

Lilian Corindon is dear but not really necessary to Cyril: "he had been born alone, must die alone, and could find the happiness best suited to his soul by hiding from his fellow-creatures lost in self" (474). After ruining George and disappointing Lilian, though saving one of his two sisters, Cyril returns at last to his boyhood path of the "Green Way" to live in a state of peace at Blue Violet: nature "he loved–what woman in the world could match that moon-mist, so lovely, so gentle, above all so silent?" (508). Does this resemble the self-involved and sinful "confinement of the self" that the celibate priest in "By Violence" must overcome to find a vicarious joy in the birth of a cottager's child (*Written . . . Rain*18)? Do we have a moral mystery and subtle ethical puzzle to be worked out as to how Cyril or George should be construed? Are they merely garden-variety fallible mortals? Or at the end when Cyril fails at human interactions but finds happiness in living alone in Nature, forgetting his past errors, is he mortally selfish?

Cyril's intensely personal struggle may be understood from a psychological point of view if this is meant to be a story about a homoerotic attachment all but unrecognized by the two men themselves. If so, then Cyril's ultimate misstep is not cowardice but inadequate coping techniques arising from a failure to recognize how unconscious gender anxieties feed social fears and the forces of control. That would make this novel, over and above its power of poetic mysticism, most exceptional for 1912. Lilian says:

> "I love you, Cyril; yet, perhaps, I do not love you as George does."
>
> "If that is true I do not understand it."
>
> "You cannot understand George. Even father cannot. I love you as much as I can, yet I doubt if my love is equal to his; and I believe George loves you as he never will, and never can, love any woman. . . . You know what sacrifice a man will make for the girl he dearly loves. I am certain George would make such sacrifice for you." (182)

Lilian's love of Cyril lacks commitment because heas well cannot summon up the passion to love her. His sister Eva says to him: "She came out of her garden to give herself to you, and now she has gone back to the garden. Your path is the same as hers, but it is too narrow for you both to walk along it side by side" (501). And Cyril's sister Eva will not marry George for the same basic reason Lilian does not accept Cyril–a failure of heterosexual passion. Bidding goodbye to George, Cyril says about marriage: "Love is the leading incident of life, but not the greatest thing, not necessary as the best for you and for me. Something will come out of Nature for each of us: to you from the fields; to me from the solitude" (506, 500). One senses, more than perceives, an autobiographical undercurrent in this conclusion.As Trevena's publisher had disclosed, "he often retires to a lonely little cottage on the top of a hill" where he "lives absolutely alone with his dogs." Trevena wrote of Gregory Breakback in *Heather* that he "had life still to win; for it is a chamber-mate that makes life, and loneliness is life decapitated" (154). This loneliness also is much like that of Burrough who says: "I listen to the wind; I play with my shadow; I watch the lamplight for some hours nightly" (*Pixy* 65). But although Trevena comments on Boodles that her lonely life on Dartmoor after the death of her father is "unwholesome at any age" (*Furze* 297), yet such solitude may also "work strangely upon the imagination" to foster creativity(*Menotah* 16).

Readers who feel Cyril's selfish career deserves "the completeness of an immediate compensating punishment" are reminded by Grace Colbron that such literary conclusions are not typical of life (327). But is nature for Cyril merely a mistress who will not make moral judgments–a form of escape, something in which to lose himself? Grappling with how to understand this denouement, the reader might find that Cyril's word "solitude" (506) brings to mind what Paul Tillich, one of the greatest theologians of the twentieth century, has said; namely, that solitude is a moral principle:

> Our language has wisely .. . created the word "loneliness" to express the pain of being alone. And it has created the word "solitude" to express the glory of being alone. Although, in daily life, we do not always distinguish these words, we should do so consistently and thus deepen our understanding of our human predicament. . . . Loneliness can be conquered only by those who can bear solitude. We have a natural desire for solitude because we are men. We want to feel what we are–namely, alone–not in pain and horror, but with joy and

> courage. There are many ways in which solitude can be sought and experienced. And each way can be called "religious," if it is true, as one philosopher said, that "religion is what a man does with his solitariness.". . .
>
> One of these ways is the desire towards the silence of nature. We can speak without voice to the trees and the clouds and the waves of the sea. Without words they respond through the rustling of leaves and the moving of clouds and the murmuring of the sea. This solitude we can have, but only for a brief time. For we realize that the voices of nature cannot ultimately answer the questions in our mind. Our solitude in nature can easily become loneliness, and so we return to the world of man. . . .
>
> And perhaps when we ask–what is the innermost nature of solitude? we should answer–the presence of the eternal upon the crowded roads of the temporal. It is the experience of being alone but not lonely, in view of the eternal presence that shines through the face of the Christ, and that includes everybody and everything from which we are separated. In the poverty of solitude all riches are present. Let us dare to have solitude–to face the eternal, to find others, to see ourselves. (Tillich 30)

Note that Tillich is not quite as confident about nature providing an ultimate answer as is Squire Tucker, although one may well see why a wonderfully social, international theologian and preacher, would want the human face. But Tillich's masters, those German Idealists of the previous century, excluded from no place this transcendental presence that "includes everybody and everything from which we are separated." Indeed, Squire Tucker had told Cyril earlier:

> "Think of the past only to repent of it," he said, "and when repented of let it lie as dead. The obstacles to your progress have been great; mercy will be dealt you in proportion. Your first stage will be loneliness, and you must make the best use of it; the second stage will be desire for sympathy, and at last will come love for the best thing in life, which to most is a woman, to a few Nature. You are among the few." (*Wintering Hay* 316)

The reader no longer has a subtle ethical puzzle or a moral mystery to work out as to how to judge Cyril. The conclusion supports his solitude as principled, a choice, however, the author perhaps for personal reasons does not expatiate upon. If Cyril's preference is unlike Father Leigh's for a self-sufficient life in an artificial rose garden, then conversely Cyril must be reaching out tosomething that is "loved and loving," losing himself in nature's infinite Mind and achieving thereby a consummate consciousness of Being.

CHAPTER 9

SLEEPING WATERS (1913)

The argument for *Sleeping Waters* as a deservedly fine intellectual classic that should be added to the canon may well begin with what two of its original trans-Atlantic reviewers said of it. A review in the *New York Times* begins:

> It would be difficult to find a novel more unusual or more original than this latest work of the author who chooses to be known as John Trevena. Allegory and realism, folk-lore and character-study, impressive pictures of a land strange and wild as that famous "misty mid-region of Weir"[Poe "Ulalume"], and, dominating all, a divided personality, a mind at once disordered and clairvoyant, seeing all things in unreal and twisted guises, yet sometimes penetrating to the ultimate truth, even to that truth of thought and motive which men refuse to admit to their own souls–it combines all these interests while remaining primarily a story wrought by a mystic, yet on the surface a tale susceptible of an entirely materialistic explanation. ("New Year Fiction" 53)

A month later Gordon Young wrote in the *Los Angeles Times*: "The construction of the book is very artistic and is difficult to accomplish, but apart from its structural merits 'Sleeping Waters' has high value. . . . Our admiration for this author has been expressed over and over again. There is grasp and reach and power in [his] books . . . that place their author among the foremost of the English novelists" (Young IIIa).

In his lifetime, as has been noted, Trevena was popular with discriminating readers but the mingled flow of perceptions, memories, scenes, and his poetic and philosophical style proved in later years too intellectual for mass market popularity. The *Times* reviewer had observed:

> "Sleeping Waters" is emphatically not a book for the intellectually lazy. It demands close attention and mental alertness from the reader who desires to follow its venturous attempt to

> portray–partly by means of symbolism–the complex relations of body and soul and brain in a man of "extraordinary psychological development," intensely nervous, more than a little morbid, exceptionally imaginative, who under the stress of change and shock, saw all things in strange aspects. That it is beautifully written, full of poetic passages, and contains many fascinating descriptions of the moor . . . will be regarded as a matter of course by those who have read any of the preceding books. ("New Year Fiction" 55)

How could anyone not admire in this novel Trevena's image of a nubile girl sitting on a rock, "her face detrimental to all philosophy" (*Sleeping Waters* 146-147). Or pity the celibate priest of his witticism, "A man who has never loved a woman can only half love his God" (231). Or applaud his gracious recognition in face of Protestant and Catholic antagonism that "charity is too holy to need a creed" (7). Or endorse the enlightened pragmatism of "Self-sacrifice is much the same as suicide" (5). Or chuckle when his protagonist answers a lazy farmer's charge of trespass: "I am not damaging your crop of moss by trampling on it" (277). The *New York Times* reviewer concluded his estimate by declaring that the author of *Sleeping Waters* is "unquestionably one of the most notable of living writers" ("New Year Fiction" 55).

Very much as Trevena himself had been compelled for the sake of his lungs to seek the higher elevations of Dartmoor–"which is said to have brought health to its author as to John Anger" (55)–his protagonist (whose surname is an old Norman one, pronounced "Ahn-jer") is a young priest of the slums whose selfless and continuous exposure to the poverty and polluted atmosphere of London leaves him physically exhausted and near death. For "Father Jack," Dartmoor's earth and sky become an awakening to a new life of the body and spirit: "a big rounded hill beside the village . . . healed me. It hung over my bed, breathing new life into me" (*Sleeping Waters* 180). When after four months his initial symptoms of exhaustion, pulmonary distress, and fever left him, he is allowed to go out of doors. But later, after drinking the magic "sleeping waters" of the stream Nympha (an upper world River Lethe of forgetfulness), he becomes lost in a mist. The shock of exposure from the cold damp on the moors seemingly renders Anger delirious, and from this point onwards he begins to move through a strange and wild world. Anger's fever filters objective reality through his unstable perceptions and subliminal ideational structures in which the initial baseline of daily reality is lost. He bizarrely correlates his naturopathic cure with that of his friend's Catholic ancestor in the time of Charles I. In Anger's present, with old political-religious animosities of the Civil War behind them, his Catholic and Protestant friends combined to rehabilitate "Father Jack." But although long gone, Hugh Billacott, a Royalist supporter of King Charles I in his struggle with Parliament, becomes part of Anger's present reality, a quickening prototype from ancestral history three hundred years previously whose milieu phantasmagorically returns in the present. The early seventeenth- century cavalier had been wounded, but after he drinks from the healing waters of Nympha he is so fully cured that according to the Billacott family book he engaged in an affair with his wife's lady-help, Petronel Vigar.

In this fantastic dream world that amalgamates new and old, Anger and Hugh are part of a cycle of recurrence that keeps modernity in touch with its past. In the mist, Anger stumbles upon the shelter of the beautiful river nymph, Petronel, and her demented worshiper, the boy Whippety. Whippety's father is the lawyer Curgenven, a demonic and crafty dwarf; his violent and drunken mother, Judith, is also Petronel's adoptive parent. Curgenven, hidden by piles of books or behind his revolving *trompe-l'oeil* bookcase, is not merely Anger's competitor for the prize of "Petronel" but also doubles the author's fallen self screened by the text. Anger's passion for Petronel, who is sometimes endearing but often cruel, culminates when, as a winter storm rages, she induces him to murder Judith with a hammer–a crime in the cellar of the Vigars's dark house of Stiniel where all that is demented and guilty is concentrated. Spellbound by Petronel, Anger descends to this act of brute passion, experiencing a guilt he has never before known. Yet, like John Milton's Adam, he falls to rise–from seduction by the senses to a "far better" love and beauty. Anger gains his reward only after he awakens from the spell of the sleeping waters. In delirium Anger believes he has committed murder, but the act in reality was a killing of his perilous enslavement to the elemental forces of nature. He and Trevena are now alike, weighed by the shadows of experience and knowledge yet open to new life. As

Petronel vanishes upon the moor, Anger finds in her place Mary, daughter of the Wiggaton's, who had been his sisterly London companion-in-charity. Hitherto, Mary's love for the saintly "Father Jack" had remained necessarily unspoken, and he had refused to acknowledge even to himself his love for her. Mary Wiggaton embodies the creative powers of Petronel yet is herself an actual woman, reconciling in one person nature with grace, the tangible with the inexpressible infinite.

Trevena's novel appeared just before the beginning of the First World War, and its London scenes foreshadowed post-War disillusionment and alienation as evinced in the Expressionist and Surrealist art that was to come in the 1920s. In *Sleeping Waters,* Trevena relates the history of Anger's treatment and convalescence via the emerging generic possibilities of magical realism. Among aesthetic modes seeking to reinvest life with an intrinsic enchantment, magical realism opened up an in-between or hidden space within an early twentieth-century technology and consumerism that had lost its contact with the numinous. Although the phrase *magical realism* may have first originated with artistic Surrealism, the mode itself is typical of an earlier neo-Romantic concern with the mind's subconscious or non-rational relationships to the external world, its merging of the marvelous with the ordinary. Earlier, a tenet of Symbolism, itself indebted to an even earlier neo-Platonic mysticism, held that literature ought to hint at deeper realities hidden within ordinary appearances. In 1913, Trevena's original readers assumed that a narrative time-line or sequence should bring pattern to events and move toward the protagonist's confronting his personal problems and their resolution. But Anger's escape into the unpredictable mythic events of Dartmoor is more equivocal than conventional mimesis which keeps a sharp narrative line drawn on the page between the marvelous and the probable. By combining dream with fact Trevena's novel problematizes the reader's understanding of Anger's situation: what is his dream, what is his reality? How magical or how real is this magical realism? And what is the generic difference between this literary aesthetic and fantasy or mysticism?

Trevena told Myrtle Henry that "mysticism has always been a part of my nature: I mean a feeling of contact with other lands unseen." In his younger days, he says, he "underwent some remarkable experiences (spiritual you might call them) which could hardly be described and cannot be forgotten" (3). His word in *Sleeping Waters* for Anger's uncanny contact with the fantastic lurking within the ordinary is "enchantment," from the Old French *enchanter* and Latin *incantare*, to bewitch or cast a magical spell by song. Trevena's story begins with classical realism; but to redress limitations of the ordinary he employs strategies to subvert reality, presenting images and scenes in unfamiliar or uncanny ways to accent a latent and mysterious power within the flat, the jejune, the modern. This balance between magic and realism in which one ontological level supplements the other (present here more than a half century before Gabriel García Márquez's *One Hundred Years of Solitude*, 1967, the most celebrated work of magical realism) opens windows on unsuspected possibilities–not the possibility that the fantastic may be *literally* true, but the possibility that things as we assume them to be (and of which we often despair) might be somehow otherwise. The appeal of magical realism lies in its capacity for liberating readers from the "reality rut" of daily life, bringing them for a time into fruitful contact with emotion, imagination, and "the unknown" so that when they return to their trades and professions, they have a richer context for their lives' possibilities.

In a farsighted review of *Sleeping Waters*, Cornelia Van Pelt is able to appreciate the impact of this avant-garde narrative technique:

> Months in bed under careful nursing build up the priest's body, but his mind is still asleep. Flesh reigns and desires unknown before awaken. He finds the Water of Nympha and drinks thereof. What happens after that is told with a consummate art which we do not recognise at first. We feel irritation at the jerky, jumbled style of the narrative until the truth comes as a delicious shock, a decided sensation, and we see how artfully, or rather how artistically, the style fitted the impression to be made. We are as much at sea as is "Father Jack," and cry confused "what here is dream and what is waking?" Was Petronel, the sun-browned maiden, really only a figure in a dream, or was she the Spirit of Dartmoor revealed to a mortal for a time? . . . This is done not as seeking sensational effects but written with a virility that seems like the

> natural exuberance of an imagination controlled only by the limits of literary style. (Van Pelt 99)

The power of *Sleeping Waters* is owing to just this merging of the subjective–the unconscious or intuitive side that cannot be adequately apprehended through empirical reason or sense–with the objective. When describing John Anger's search for the waters of Nympha, we read:

> "I grow wiser," declared Anger, as he found himself in a solitude which might have been unexplored territory, so entirely was it lacking in every sign of human occupation, and looked upon a region of furze and heather, shining bogs, and stony upland. . . . Being an imaginative man, he could not wander there alone and keep romance away. The tales he had listened to in childhood became retold; falsehood and truth were mingled together; history and myth kissed each other. The folklore, which Jonas the singer stubbornly believed in, the rites and mysteries of his own Church, the deed from the Abbot of Buckfast, the mystic powers of consecrated water, became to his mind the chapters of a story which his own life was to continue, a dream-like story to which he must add realities. (*Sleeping Waters* 44)

One senses Trevena is working within a modernist aesthetic, achieving some of the striking effects of modernism or postmodernism, whether they be the time-lapse of sleep in Virginia Woolf's *Orlando* (1928) or the delusions of Vladimir Nabokov's "Terra Incognita" (1931) in which the baseline of reality vanishes.

But one need not appeal only to modish examples. Trevena's intellectual style and visionary reality had impeccable historical credentials derived from late-nineteenth-century Idealism–neo-Platonic philosophy, Swedenborgian occultism, German Romanticism, and British mysticism from William Blake to the *fin-de-siècle* W.B. Yeats. When Arthur Symons connected Olive Schreiner's 1891 *Dreams* with the French Symbolists' mystical correspondences, such or comparable surreal prose also lay behind Trevena's techniques. And, as in Walter Pater's visionary aestheticism, Trevena mastered the gem-like impression, fragmentary yet entire in itself: "A woman stood bareheaded, calm, but in an agony. A gaslight, placed behind a bottle of green liquid in a chemist's shop, made her face terrible. She stood and swayed; and following the direction of her gaze towards a newsvendor's across the way, Anger saw in that needless horror of green light the latest evening paper rumour; and a ship had been wrecked; and she was a widow who stood there staring" (112). The accidental play of fallen light might be Pater's; the absinthe hues surely leapt from the palette of Toulouse Lautrec. Subsequent to *Sleeping Waters*, and recalling also the setting of *Heather*, one of the closest affinities with Trevena's evocative imagery and avant-garde aesthetics was Thomas Mann's philosophical masterwork, *The Magic Mountain* (1924), a novel of inner growth or a *buildungs-roman* of an everyman-figure, Hans, who spends seven years at an isolated tuberculosis sanatorium at Davos in the Swiss Alps. Is he truly sick or simply trapped by the magical rocks and snow? As a microcosm for European life just before the transformative catastrophe of World War I, Mann's retrospective setting allegorizes the spiritual and psychological illnesses of a pre-war society. He pits ideologies of modern science and cultural progress against occult medievalism and mystical communism; and he explores the passage of time and its relationships with space, body, and mind, including Hans' awakening to a life of the senses with desire for "the eternal feminine."

Sleeping Waters opens with the indictment that Exeter has destroyed its urban antiquities for the sake of commercialization, making money being more important than any touristic value inhering in tradition. At first, Anger naively dismisses "old traditions" as "worth nothing" and impulsively exaggerates: "Modernity is unlawful in my church" (26). The narrative chooses "rasped" and "clashed" to describe the past's incompatibility with the present. This question whether the old is worth keeping especially relates to Curgenven's scheme to replace the quaint village of Youlstone with resort villas. (Youlstone and Trevena's other place-names, which may exist somewhere in the West Country, are fictional for Dartmoor. Youlstone is Belstone; South Wyld is South Zeal, which also had a grand old residence converted to an inn; and Riversmeet is Okehampton at the confluence of the East and West Okement.) The farmers' connection to their land was the essence of their livelihoods, culture, and identity; but farms that not long before seemed of little outside value were now being sought by investors for real estate development–perhaps accompanied with new livelihood opportunities for the commoners but more likely only a net loss. The year this novel was published, for example, the Okehampton Golf Club, self-described as "The jewel in the heart of Devon," was built in an ancient deer park on the banks of the West Okement River in Dartmoor. As previously noted, Trevena for a time as a young man had clerked in a law firm until its partners discovered he wrote poetry. Before he was thereupon promptly fired, he likely had learned the facts of modern commercial land development and the fraud issues that *Sleeping Waters* spotlights. Mr. Odyorne in *Heather* foreshadows Curgenven, the diabolic money-lender, who hustles loans to these naive commoners who are unaware that they are losing their independence and selling their souls to the devil. It is not just "the silent moor mortgaged to winter" (199) or Petronel who is "in the power of a humpbacked dwarf" (154). Anger observes: "It seems to me the commoners of Youlstone are children, taking pocket-money from their master, and never dreaming of a day of settlement. . . . To accept a loan, knowing it means the sacrifice of a home, is the act of a madman" (194-195). But the stubborn villagers, bound by ignorance and traditional pride, refuse the help they so desperately need, even when Anger offers them an opportunity.

When he first sets out for Dartmoor the only myths or magic in Anger's life are artificial and unimaginative clichés, though kindly meant. His London friend Billacott informs him that he will find "Buttercups and daisies instead of smuts and chimneys. A parish full of larks and butterflies in place of sweated seamstresses and penny-toy merchants. That's the poetry of it, Father Jack–and I shall visit you with sonnets in the summer" (9). Trevena compares such pastoral fantasy to real-life social concerns, the harsh rural life that in *A Pixy in Petticoats* he had called "unutterably drab and dirty in reality" (87) and that in *Sleeping Waters* he presents as the choking backwardness of Dartmoor from which "those who have profited by education emigrate, while the old and the dull stay on; and tradition dies hard with them" (184). Although the commoners lead grueling lives, their formidable ignorance nevertheless is cause for satiric treatment. In *A Pixy in Petticoats*, Ann's milking stool emblematizes stubborn rustic tradition. Willum recites his mother's comment why her cow is in the middle of the road:

"'Mother milked 'en here, so did her mother, so did hers, and I be going to long as I lives.'. . . Mrs. Cobbledick had always milked her cows in the middle of the road, and she intended to persevere in that practice so long as she might live. . . . For it had never occurred to her that it would be easier to shift the stool than to place the cow beside it" (38, 302).

Although the satiric authorial voice may polish the narrative's factual fundamentals, the underlying bone structure of Trevena's realism is undistorted and largely true to life; anduntil the illusion of representing reality is shattered by artful narrative devices, there is nothing magical or mythic in satire of political, business, religious, or educational affairs. Like the bizarre rocks of the moor and its flora, the whimsical or idiosyncratic dwellers on it are seriously comic. Certainly there is none of the bucolic artificiality of Phillpotts's characterizations. Trevena's covert autobiography is given an extra twist when one considers that the Anglican clergyman, Mr. Hanson, undoubtedly is yet another a satiric pen-portrait of his adoptive uncle. Even Trevena's personal political views on the currently seething conflict between labor and capital are included–the "great unrest" with strikes upon a scale unique in British history, pronounced by the *London Times* to be "the greatest catastrophe that has threatened the country since the Spanish Armada" ("Coal Strike" 9). He indirectly criticizes "King Socialism" and the mass turmoil in urban workplaces around the country, commenting on the primitive life-ways of Dartmoor where "within each parish communism flourished" (44)–only because the commoners do not know they are practicing it.

In 1910, Trevena had published a story, "By Violence," that one might call a prologue to the magic of*Sleeping Waters*. Father Searall has not found fulfillment in service to his Church. He retires early to seek the meaning of his life in the peace and innocence of nature but discovers he first must affirm death and violence as constituents of the earth's ceaselessly interacting antinomies of generation and decay: "he awoke from the sleep of death and felt the spring. The winter was over and past, the time of the opening of flowers had come, and the voice of creation stirred upon the garden; and the change had been wrought by violence" (*Written . . . Rain* 28-29). In *Sleeping Waters,* the awakening of the religious self to new life revolves around this inevitable violence.

Although Victorian and Edwardian novels portray numerous Anglican clergymen, not surprisingly Roman Catholic priests are less in evidence, and few of these are fictional protagonists. The closest predecessor Searall and Anger's vocation and transformation may be Prior Saint-Jean in Walter Pater's "Apollo in Picardy" (1893). In Pater's story, this medieval monk and his servant are sent to the country "for the benefit of his body's health, a little impaired at last by long intellectual effort. . . . The Prior and his companion, were come in contact for the first time in their lives with the power of untutored natural impulse, of natural inspiration" (146, 156). Similarly on Dartmoor, where the Bronze Age quite literally meets the twentieth century, neolithic ruins and pagan beliefs co-exist with the living present. The psychological transitions of both the Prior and Anger portray an escape from "overwrought spiritualities" into the "ancient life of the senses" with "some subtle reminiscence of older gods" (Pater, "Poems by Morris" 307-308). In Heinrich Heine's "The Gods in Exile" (1853), Pater found this fantasy of reincarnated Greek deities banished from Olympus by the advent of Christianity. This conceit was cited also in the anonymous source Trevena extensively drew upon,"The Pleasant Land of Devon" (431); and it serves as an allegory of the pagan-Christian competition between sense and spirit for the protagonist's soul. Pater's Apollyon is "immersed in, or actually a part of, that irredeemable natural world" which the Prior dreads to encounter. His "unnatural magic," potentially "secret evil," and "heathen understanding with the dark realm of matter" flouts conventional neo-Platonism that feared contamination of the spirit by the lust of the eye (Pater, "Apollo" 158-159).

Arthur Conan Doyle's *The Hound of the Baskervilles* (1902), based on the "West-Country legend" of a spectral whist hound on the moor ("Pleasant Land of Devon" 431), may come closest to anticipating Trevena's personifications of evil upon the night moor, less in his terrorizing *tour de force* of "the enormous coal-black hound" with glowing eyes and fire in its mouth than in the Grimpen mire, a hidden destroyer that swallows ponies and people–a force of nature like Petronel, queen of the underworld, "who gathers all things mortal with cold immortal hands" (Swinburne). Just as Pater's figure of Apollyon is "an embodiment of all those genial influences of earth and sky," so the classical river nymph, Petronel (*nympha* means bride or water spirit, an elemental deity), becomes the mythological embodiment of Dartmoor's streams and rocky outcrops (her medieval name is the feminine of Peter, from L. *petra*, "rock"). Certainly both Pater's portrait and*Sleeping Waters* belong to Bulwer's "Intellectual School," given that in place of direct action their aim is portraiture, a revelation of character. Not only do they recast traditional plot in terms of sensations and forces, but sharply etched impressions are lifted above themselves as if in a dream. Trevena's literary style, too, is often similar to Pater's sensuously rich, deep, "harmonious murmur"–in "Apollo in Picardy" Apollyon *sings* (the root sense of enchantment) the monastic tithe-barn into existence.

Anger's psychopathology reflects his priestly iconology in subconscious fantasies and fragments from the darker side of his psyche–mythical figures, bewildering scenes, and ominous incidents–with perplexing flashbacks from his illusions to reality: "The sun in its course cast upon the ground the shadow of a point of rock, . . . the blot of black suggested a limbless trunk, a mighty pair of shoulders with a strong head midway" (141). Trevena seemingly alludes to early psychological experiments where blots, leading to the Rorschach inkblot test in 1921, were used to assess subconscious obsessions, here the diabolic in the shape of Curgenven. By tapping into Nympha's dreams, Anger plunges into ancient mythic patterns and historical lives without the ball and chain of objective constraints. Somewhat earlier just before the turn of the century, the British physician, Neil Macleod, reported experiments in the *British Medical Journal* with bromide-induced narcosis, giving psychopharmacology one of its earliest successes in the form of deep sleep therapy. Trevena's plot seemingly substitutes Nympha's waters in the place of Macleod's pharmaceutical doses. A comparable idea of "medical dreams" used to identify "the maladies of the soul" dated back to the ancient Greek Aesculapius (Pater, *Marius* 1:29). And when in the late nineteenth century philosophy and experimental physiology ceded the study of human emotions and motives to the new discipline of psychology, the intricacies of the mind classified by Aristotle's four archetypal "temperaments"–the phlegmatic, choleric, sanguine, and melancholic–reemerged as Sigmund Freud's and Carl Jung's psychological patterns of behavior. Jung's ideal of personal wholeness restated Aristotle's balance of "humors" as thinking, feeling, sensation, and intuition. From ancient and medieval times febrile delirium had been described by Celsus, Hippocrates, Procopius and others as a mix of intense insomnia and waking dreams, the patient exhibiting intervals of incipient lucidity between states of dreaming hallucination. Such observations of delusion culminated popularly in the work of Trevena's contemporary, Sigmund Freud, who observed that retreat into illusions and an alienation from reality is comparable to a waking dream or a psychosis in which the brain refuses to subordinate its neurotic dreams to what actually is. Parallels between delusion and dream suggested a new diagnostic category known as "the clouding of consciousness," symbolized in *Sleeping Waters* by Anger's confusion in the mist about his immediate surroundings.

Another important influence on Trevena's thinking has already been mentioned in earlier chapters: Frederic Myers' *Human Personality* in which he discusses forms of personality alteration:

> it sometimes happens, as a result of shock, disease, or unknown causes, that a man or a woman experiences an alteration of character, amounting to a change of personality, which generally seems to have come on during sleep. . . . It generally disappears after a time, or alternates with the original, or *primary* personality. . . . Furthermore, . . . sometimes during apparent ordinary sleep the spirit may travel away from the body, and may bring back a memory, more or less confused, of what it has seen in this clairvoyant excursion. This may indeed happen for brief flashes during waking moments also. But ordinary sleep seems to help the process; and deeper states of sleep–spontaneous or induced–seem still further to facilitate it. (1:xxi, 2:193)

In such delusional dream states, actual stimuli are given additional, bizarre significance, often unfolding at a different tempo and in a sequence dissociated from actual cause and effect.

These subjectivities of time and space were ratified pragmatically, even before Einsteinian relativity, by the new velocities of the railroad which expanded mobility in space and compressed travel times, while such avant-garde technology in the 1870s as the time-lapse photography of Eadweard Muybridge's running horses overturned the limits of reality and provided new insights into the enigma of the individual moment. Additionally, the temporal and spatial scales of geology and biology combined with the unprecedented global spread of the British empire to "psychologize" the scope and feel of things in which the baseline of daily reality seemed lost. Anger recalls sleep-lapse episodes in legends that collapsed or telescoped time and place,such as those of the monk Felix so enchanted by the song of a bird that a hundred years passed seemingly in a single hour, or of the sleeping Finn (a Celtic hero-legend) orof "Thorn Rose," the Grimm Brother's sleeping princess. Sleep, says Lord Byron in "The Dream," is a boundary world in which dreams become:

> A portion of ourselves, ...
> They make us what we were not.
> . . . . . . What are they?
> Creations of the mind?—
> . . . . . . in itself a thought,
> A slumbering thought, is capable of years,
> And curdles a long life into one hour.

Dreams become subjective mindscapes, perceptions driven by instinct. Anger's is thus not the story of a man but the story of a man's mind–not events as they happened, but as a mad priest imagines they occurred.

With narrative richness, Trevena invests the *dramatis personae* of *Sleeping Waters* with the elemental forces of the moor and the ancient myths of the seasonal cycles, fulfilling the novel's theme of"the death of an old life, the beginning of a new" (8). In the nineteenth century the study of comparative mythology owed much to F. Max Müller, a linguistic ethnologist, who hypothesized the origin of culture as lying in a "mythopoeic age" in which the diurnal and seasonal "solar drama" was reenacted by a young hero whose death is "suggested by the Sun, dying in all his youthful vigor, either at the end of a day, conquered by the powers of darkness, or at the end of the sunny season, stung by the thorn of winter" (Müller 2: 107, 140). A paragraph in the "Brother and Sister" chapter in *Sleeping Waters* seems almost a fictionally poetic restatement of Müller's theme (138-139). Among the most influential of Müller's successors in systematizing ritual and myth were E.B. Tylor, whose *Primitive Culture* (1871) became for its day the standard in cultural anthropology, and Sir James Frazer's *The Golden Bough* (1890). Their references amply document a plethora of seasonal myths of the earth in its changes–such as a light and dark duality in the sun and moon gods, Baal and Ashtoreth, or the summer and winter phases of Dionysus or Demeter in Greek mythology. Through her twin daughters Kore/Persephone, Demeter the "wrinkled woman," who "grows young again every spring yet is of great age,"personifies this cyclic pattern. She gives birth, fertilizes the fields and clothes nature; but she is also a grim goddess, cruel and destructive, who revokes her life-giving power and brings barrenness and death. Demeter in her cruel phase as the "mistress and manager of men's shades" slays her child but concurrently is "mourning her loss." (Pater, *Greek Studies* 105, 94). In its Mesopotamian variant, as midsummer climaxes, the springtime consort of the goddess is slain. The mother-goddess, as the personification of plant life and of sexual love, then enters the nether world to rescue him, and at each of the seven gates through which she passes, some of her clothing and adornments are removed until she passes through the last gate naked. The earth continues infertile until the goddess reemerges, arrayed again like spring in her full splendor.

Petronel, the fairy-tale sleeping princess or "elf-maiden," is this twofold seasonal goddess of summer and winter personifying Demeter's daughters. In her summer phase, Petronel is the nymph of the magic waters, a counterpart to Pater's Apollyon in "Apollo in Picardy" who at first is the Apollonian god of fecundity, comically exaggerated in Trevena's novel by Bobby Billacott, a bibulous incarnation of summertime life in the green sap. But autumn initiates her period of exile in the underworld, the provenance of Anger's troubled delusions. Apollyon in this latter phase "accidentally" kills the Prior's companion, Hyacinth, with a discus, figure of the seasonal cycle. Similarly, in winter Petronel becomes the violent and sorrowing princess of death. She is the cold land epitomized by her absent "drowned" brother, whom she eventually confesses she killed and who is buried in the crypt-like cellar of Stinial (378). Petronel's controlling step-mother, the "dark witch," embodies winter's fierce madness. Curgenven is an elemental dwarf-god of the earth and of the dark unconscious, a Hades-like figure holding Petronel in his power. Whippety is Petronel's wordless "familiar," son of Curgenven and the witch. And the novel's protagonist, Anger, aspires to be Petronel's reborn fraternal double, her sun-consort of springtime renewal. Possibly the vegetation myth closest to the turbulent John Anger-Petronel Vigar kinship is the Egyptian story of the twins Isis and Osiris as recounted by Plutarch. Brother and sister began their intimacy in the womb; in maturity Seth/Typhon kills Osiris and dismembers him; Isis then collects the fragments of Osiris's body that originally had been cast into a river. Because his "genital member" had been eaten by fish, his impotence emblematizes the sterility of winter. When Anger offers himself to Petronel as her reincarnated "brother" and divine consort, she resists, owing to her self-division between vanished summer and tyrannical winter as well as to his clerical celibacy and illness, like the debilitating sterility of Osiris who waits among the dead until the coming of spring when Isis resurrects him as her partner.

Trevena's indefinite "ground situation" (as metaphysicians would call it) and his novel's multiple "planes of action" (as a literary critic might say) deny that a person lives solely in one experiential level of reality.At the end of *Sleeping Waters,* Anger asserts, less grandiloquently than Prospero in *The Tempest*, "now that the enchantment has been removed things are changed. You must know, Mr. Billacott, I have been all my life a great reader of mystical romances. The stories which above all else have impressed themselves upon my fancy are those of the *Arabian Nights*" (436). In Scherazade's famous chain of never-ending tales, the imagination of the vizier's daughter keeps her alive in her "real" world telling stories–a self-conscious reference *in* the fiction to the Romantic irony *of* the fiction. When the author or his concerns intrude upon the fictional presentation of life as it really is–i.e., as literary conventions give the illusion of "reality"–its representational veracity for the reader is impeached. In *Furze the Cruel*, Trevena had described Boodles as caught in a script that another consciousness seems to have written for her, the outcome of which she cannot control. The author himself steps in to overrule the "compositor-ogres" whose realistic story-ending, he says, he will not endorse. A gentler authorial presence in *Sleeping Waters* entangles Anger's personality in incidents and psyches from earlier cultural texts, disrupting the stability of realist narration by shifting among these frames or levels of reference. Trevena especially cites Shelley's tragedy, *The Cenci* (1820), in which "Petronel played the tragic part of Beatrice," victim of incestuous rape, and Anger plays Cenci's brutal "assassin" (253). A more indirect strategy of literary quotation had been used in *Pixy* when Burrough described himself in love had he asked: "How many would confess to the initials they had carved on beech-trees?" (34). Trevena's readers might recall Shakespeare's *As You Like It*, in which Orlando would "carve on every tree / The fair, the chaste, and unexpressive she" (3.2.9-10).In *Sleeping Waters,* Anger's life-changing infatuation with the seasonal goddess Petronel recapitulates the *topos* of Lucius's transfiguration in Apuleius's *Golden Ass* afterwards re-embodied by the ass-headed Nick Bottom in *A Midsummer Night's Dream* ("The eye of man hath not heard, the ear of man hath not seen . . . what my dream was" [4. 1]). But inasmuch as Bottom's speech has travestied 1 Corinthians 2:9 ("Eye hath not seen, nor ear heard. . . ."), the affirmation of religious revelation from ancient Palestine has been turned by North African comical witchcraft and Renaissance clowning into twentieth-century Dartmoor's enchantment of a man delusively but chasteningly in love with a supernatural spirit.

When the vanishing of Anger's hallucinations resets life within his original unenchanted reality, Trevena's readers, having been taken in by the realism of his delusions, are as likely disoriented as Anger himself. The dream has argued for its internal and surreal representations as a primary reality so convincingly that any return from those illusions to sanity is a shock. The Dartmoor dream-figures as previously encountered are now discovered to be nothing like Anger's anagogic personalities: toward the end of his dream Curgenven is killed, fittingly buried by Whippety in a collapse of earth and rock; yet after this dream dissolves, Curgenven in the outer "real" storyline frame is still alive in Riversmeet, no longer the devil, only an imperfect man. But most startling is that when Anger's delusions are remitted and his pre-morbid level of functioning returns, the original familiar urban life is not returned to its *sole* position of ontological primacy or dominance. Because Anger's formerly unacknowledged desires and his enchantment have been experienced under the guise of real-time sensory stimuli, as if in a virtual world, the aftereffects of this subversive vision carry back into his sane, rational personality as clairvoyance; and he adjusts his perceptions accordingly. This scandal–that the fantastic is not an empty echo but actually may fashion quotidian reality–had been used to good effect earlier in H.G.Wells's *Time Machine* (1895) in which his time traveler returned from the future to Victorian London with Weena's actual flower petals. So effective was this device that in *Perelandra* (1943), C. S. Lewis copied itwhen his protagonist Ransom returned from Venus–with never a hint of his disapproval of Wells's scientific agnosticism.

Thus when Trevena's story resets to its primary frame of reality, Anger's previous dreams provide him insights very much like axiomatic and intuitive *gnosis,* knowledge of the personal secrets of Dartmoor's inhabitants previously hidden from everyone but God. Frederic Myers speaks of hallucinatory perceptions "which are *veridical*–which are . . . in some way generated by some event outside the percipient's mind, so that their correspondence with the event conveys some new fact, in however obscure a form." This "bringing news to the percipient of actual facts outside his own organism . . . makes the study of inward vision no mere curiosity, but rather the opening of an inlet into forms of knowledge to which we can assign no bound" (1: 229; 239). Similarly, in *Wintering Hay,*Squire Tucker's knowledge of Cyril's secret guilt is impossible to explain apart from a mystic awareness. In terms of Trevena's contemporary literary contexts, Anger's mountain sojourn has boldly challenged the premises of realism and naturalism that humans exist in one and only one sensory environment, their destiny delimited wholly by heredity and objective circumstance without a spiritual dimension. For Trevena, the enchantment that underlies life pulls reality toward what he calls a "magnificent realism" that opens a "supernatural door" to "the spirit realm" (*Written . . . Rain* 340).

Bibliography

Note: Henham/Trevena's fiction is under "Trevena" but the name under which it was published is supplied parenthetically after the title. Only the uncollected short fiction not included in either of the two story collections below will be listed.

A

"American History." *New York Times.* 28 January 1912: BR 44.
"Among the Authors." *New York Times.* 2 January 1909: 22.
"Another Story of Dartmoor by John Trevena," rev. of *Granite. New York Times.* 23 August 1914: BR 357.

B

Beauvoir, Simone de. *Quand prime le spirituel* [*When Things of the Spirit Come First*].Paris: *Éditions Gallimard,* 1979.
Beeson, Mark. "Devon Literature at the Turn of the Millennium." *Transactions of theDevonshire Association.* Vol. 132 (2000): 161-179.
Bennett, Arnold. *Books and Persons.* London: Chatto & Windus, 1917.
"Books and the War." *New York Times.*21 March 1915: BR 104.
"Brief Notes of Stories which Repay Attention," revs. of *Granite* and *Wintering Hay. Brooklyn Daily Eagle.* 21 November 1914: * 7.
Bulwer-Lytton, Edward. *The Last of the Barons.* London: Saunders & Otley, 1843.

C

Camus, Albert. *The Myth of Sisyphus and Other Essays.*New York: Knopf, 1955.
Carew, Richard. *Survey of Cornwall.* London: J. Faulder, 1811.
"Causerie." *New York Times.* 7 February 1915: BR 44.
"Charming Arminel," rev. of *Arminel. Des Moines Daily News.* 29 May 1909: 4.
"Coal Strike and the Public." *London Times.* 26 February 1912: 9.
Colbron, Grace Isabel. "Nine Books of the Month," rev. of *Wintering Hay. Bookman* (November 1914): 327.
Cooper, Frederic Taber. *Some English Story Tellers.* New York: H. Holt, 1912.
"Current Fiction." *The Evening Post* (New York). 30 January 1909: 7.

D

Dibble, Samuel W. "Literary: An Unusual Novel," rev. of *Heather. Atlanta Constitution.* 14 June 1909: 4.
Doyle, Arthur Conan. *The Hound of the Baskervilles.* Leipzig: Tauchnitz, 1902.

E

Edgett, E. F. *Boston Evening Transcript.* 6 March 1909: 7.
---------. *Boston Evening Transcript,* rev. of *Granite.* 26 August 1914:18.
---------. *Boston Evening Transcript.* 17 October 1914: 8.

F

"Fiction." *Athenæum*, rev. of *Furze*. 30 November 1907: 683-84.
"Fiction." *Academy*, rev. of *Furze.*16 October 1907: 66-68.

G

Galbraith. "Literary London's Current Gossip," rev. of *Heather. New York Times (Saturday Review of Books*). 18 July 1908: BR402.
General Register Office. Entry of Birth, Beatrice Pentreath, 15 January 1880, Devon.
--------. Entry of Marriage, Charles Arthur Hall and Beatrice Pentreath, 6 September 1904, Cornwall.
--------. Entry of Marriage, Ernest George Henham and Selina Rose McDonald, 28 July 1910, London.
--------. Entry of Death, Thomas Ernest George Henham, 3 April 1948, Dorset.
--------. Entry of Death, Selina Rose Henham, 18 February 1960, Bournemouth.
Greene, Brian. *The Fabric of the Cosmos*. New York: Vintage Books, 2004.

H

Hardy, Thomas. "The Dorsetshire Labourer." *Longman's Magazine* (July 1883): 252-269.
--------. "General Preface to the Wessex Edition of 1912." *Tess of the d'Urbervilles*. Ed. Sarah Maier. Peterborough, Canada: Broadview Press, 2002.
Hawker, Robert Stephen. *Footprints of Former Men in Far Cornwall*. London: John Lane, 1903.
Henham, Ernest G. See Trevena, John.
Henry, Myrtle C. *John Trevena*. Diss. University of Pennsylvania. Philadelphia: Privately Printed, 1935.
Holmes,Richard. *Coleridge: Early Visions 1772-1804*. London: Hodder & Stoughton, 1989.
Huckel, Oliver. *Through England with Tennyson*. New York: Chautauqua Press, 1914.
Hunt, Robert. *Popular Romances of the West of England*. London: Chatto & Windus, 1865.

J

James, Henry. *Selected Letters of Henry James to Edmund Gosse*. Ed. Rayburn S. Moore. Baton Rough: Louisiana State U.P., 1988.
--------. *The Letters*. Ed. Percy Lubbock. New York: Scribner's & Sons, 1920.
Jerome, Jerome K. *My Life and Times*. New York and London: Harper & Bros., 1926.
"John Trevena." *The Writer: A Monthly Magazine to Interest and Help All Literary Workers*. 27:7 (July 1915): 105-106.
Jordan-Smith, Paul. *For the Love of Books*. London: Oxford U. P., 1934.
--------. *Los Angeles Times*. 29 March 1958: Part IV 9.

L

"Latest Fiction," rev. of *Wintering Hay. New York Times*. 25 October 1914: BR 459.
"Latest Works of Fiction," rev. of *Drake. New York Times*. 5 November 1916: BR 1-3.
Leclaire, Lucien. *A General Analytical Bibliography of the Regional Novelists in the British Isles 1800-1950*. Paris: *Société des Belles Lettres*, 1954.

M

Mallory, Thomas.*The History of King Arthur*. Ed. Thomas Wright. 3 vols. London: J. R. Smith [1858], 1866.
Martin, Ernest Walter. "John Trevena: A Neglected Novelist." *The West Country Magazine*. 1: 2 (Autumn 1946): 87-89.
Melville, Lewis. "John Trevena, English Novelist." *New York Times*. 21 March 1908: BR 157.
Messurier, Brian Le. "Author Who Upset His Neighbours." *Western Morning News*. 12 February 1965: 6.
Monmouth,Geoffrey. *Histories of the Kings of Britain*. Trans. Sebastian Evans. London: Dent, 1904.
Monsman, Gerald, ed. *Furze the Cruel*. By John Trevena. 1907. Kansas City: Valancourt Books, 2010.
Morrison, Duncan. *The Great Hymns of the Church*. Toronto: Hart, 1890.
Müller, Max. "Comparative Mythology" (1856). *Chips from a German Workshop*. New York: Scribner, Armstrong, 1876.
Myers, Frederic. *Human Personality and Its Survival of Bodily Death*. 2 vols. London: Longmans, Green, 1903.
"Mystic's Tale," rev. of *Bracken*. *New York Times*. 24 March 1912: BR 163.

N

"New Year Fiction," rev. of *Sleeping Waters.New York Times*. 10 January 1915: 53-55.
"News of Books." *New York Times*. 16 August 1914: BR 352.
"Novelist of Dartmoor, A: The Mystery of John Trevena's Puzzling Genius." *Current Opinion*. 57: 6 (December 1914): 429.
"Novels of Eden Phillpotts" [C. S. E.]. *The Teacher's World* (19 March 1919): 652.

O

O[xenham], E[lsie] J. "The Mystery of 'John Trevena.'" *The Cornhill Booklet*. 4:3 December 1914): 97-99.

P

Page, John L. W. "Pixies." *An Exploration of Dartmoor*. London: Seeley, 1892.
Pater,Walter. "Apollo in Picardy." *Harper's New Monthly Magazine* 87 (November 1893): 949-957.
--------. "Apollo in Picardy." *Miscellaneous Studies*. London: Macmillan, 1910: 142-171.
--------. "Poems by William Morris." *Westminster Review* 34 n.s. (October, 1868): 300-312.
--------. *Letters of Walter Pater*. Ed. Lawrence Evans. Oxford: Clarendon Press, 1970.
--------. *Marius the Epicurean*. 2 vols. London: Macmillan, 1885.
--------. *Renaissance,The*. London: Macmillan, 1910.
Peattie, Elia."Trevena's Cornish Story," rev. of *Furze.Chicago Daily Tribune*. 6 June 1908: 9.
--------. "Second of John Trevena's Moorland Trilogy is 'Heather.'" *Chicago Daily Tribune*. 29 May 1909: 12.
--------. "Among the New Books: Trevena's New Novel Strange and Menacing," rev. of *Bracken*. *ChicagoDaily Tribune*. 2 March 1912: 11.

--------. "In the Field of Literary Endeavor: Trevena's Dartmoor Story," rev. of *Wintering Hay. Chicago Daily Tribune.* 23 January 1915: 10.
Phillpotts, Eden. *Children of the Mist: A Novel.* London: A. D. Innes, 1898.
"Phillpotts Takes His Final Stroll Through Dartmoor." *New York Times.* 15 April 1923: 7-10.
"Pleasant Land of Devon, The." *The Quarterly Review* 178:356 (April 1894): 414-436.
"Powerful Novel," rev. of *Wintering Hay. Los Angeles Times.*6 December 1914: AB 4.
Prickman, J. D. "West Country Wit and Humor." *Report and Transactions of the Devonshire Association.* Vol. 30. Plymouth: W. Brendon, 1898.
"Publisher's Advertisement." *Devon and Exeter Gazette.*26 February 1909: 10.
"Publisher's Notice," rev. of *Furze. Daily Mail* as qtd. in *Bracken*(1910): [ii].
"Publisher's Notice," rev. of *Granite. Westminster Gazette* asqtd. in *Bracken* (1910): [ii].
"Publisher's Notice," rev. of*Pixy. Liverpool Courier* as qtd. in *Pixy* (Rivers' Shilling Series, 1908): [ii].

R

Rev. of *Bracken.Saturday Review.* 21 January 1911: 87.
Rev. of *Pixy. Academy.* 15 April 1907: 393.
Rev. of *Pixy. Lloyds Weekly News.*19 August 1906: 16.
Rev. of *Poems*, by Francis Thompson. *Athenæum.* 13 February 1894: 143.
Rev. of *Rejected Addresses*, by Francis Jeffrey. *Edinburgh Review.* 20: 40 (November 1812): 434-451.
Reynolds, Joshua. *The Literary Works.* Ed. H.W. Beechey. Vol. 1. London: George Bell, 1899.
Ruskin, John. *The Complete Works.* Eds. E.T. Cook and Alexander Wedderburn. Vol. 20. London: George Allen, 1905.

S

Sigfusson,Saemund. "The Song of the Sun." *The Elder Eddas.* Trans. Benjamin Thorpe.London: Norroena Society, 1906.
"Sketch of John Trevena." *Bookman.* (September 1908): 3-4.
"Some Press Opinions," rev. of *Furze. Dundee Advertiser* as qtd. in *Furze* (Rivers' Shilling Series, 1913): [ii].
"Spirit of Endurance," rev. of *Heather. New York Times.* 12 June 1909: BR 366.
Symons, Arthur. "Walter Pater." *Studies in Prose and Verse.* London: Dent, 1904.

T

Tanguy, Théophile. "John Trevena." *Mémoire présenté pour le Diplôme d'Etudes Supérieures. Université de Rennes*, 1961.
Tillich, Paul. *The Eternal Now.* New York: Charles Scribner's Sons, 1963.
Tobias, Richard. *T. E. Brown.* Boston: Twayne Publishers, 1978.
"Topics of the Week." *New York Times.* 13 December 1914: BR 566.
"Trevena, John." *Who's Who.* Chicago: Marquis Co., 1928-44.
Trevena, John. *Adventures Among Wild Flowers* (Trevena). London: Edward Arnold, 1914.
--------. *Arminel of the West* (Trevena). London: Alston Rivers, 1907.
--------. *Bonanza: A Tale of the Outside* (Henham). London: Hutchinson, 1901.
--------. *Bracken* (Trevena). London: Alston Rivers, 1910.

--------. *Captain's Furniture,The* (Trevena). London: Mills and Boon, 1916; or *A Drake by George!* New York: Alfred A. Knopf, 1916.
--------. "Cat-Eye Wife, The" (Henham). *Phil May's Annual.*14 (Winter 1902/03): 48-54.
--------. *Custom of the Manor, The* (Trevena). London: Mills and Boon, 1924.
--------. *Dartmoor House That Jack Built, The* (Trevena). London: Alston Rivers, 1909.
--------. *Feast of Bacchus, The: A Study in Dramatic Atmosphere* (Henham). London: Brown, Langham and Co., 1907.
--------. "Frog Chorus, A" (Henham). *Phil May's Annual.* 6 (Winter 1896): 16-24.
--------. *Furze the Cruel* (Trevena). London: Alston Rivers, 1907.
--------. *God, Man and the Devil* (Henham). London: Skeffington & Son, 1897.
--------. *Granite* (Trevena). London: Alston Rivers, 1909.
--------. *Heather* (Trevena). London: Alston Rivers, 1908.
--------. *Krum: A Study in Consciousness* (Henham). London: Grant Richards, 1904.
--------. "Lid, The" (Henham). [Typescript with the author's ms. corrections, n.d., 13 pgs.] New York Public Library.
--------. "Matrimonial Misadventure, A" (Henham). *Phil May's Annual.*8 (June 1898): 48-58.
--------. *Menotah: A Tale of the Riel Rebellion* (Henham). London: Skeffington & Son, 1897.
--------. "Mourning Oak, The" (Trevena). *The Weekly Tale-Teller.* 138 (23 December 1911): 1-8.
--------. *No Place Like Home* (Trevena). London: Constable and Co., 1913.
--------. *Off the Beaten Track* (Trevena). London: Mills and Boon, 1925.
--------. "Old Bailey's Wooing" (Henham). *Macmillan's Magazine.* 93: 12 N.S.(October 1906): 908-918; retitled "Froggie Would a-Wooing Go!" *Written in the Rain.*(1910): 261-277.
--------. *Pixy in Petticoats,A* (Anonymous). London: Alston Rivers, 1906.
--------. *Plowshare and the Sword: A Tale of Old Quebec, The* (Henham). London: Cassell and Co., 1903.
--------. *Raindrops* (Trevena). London: Holden and Hardingham, 1920.
--------. *Reign of the Saints, The* (Trevena). London: Alston Rivers, 1911.
--------. *Scud* (Henham). London: Burleigh, 1902.
--------. *Short Stories and Essays of Ernest George Henham* (Henham/Trevena). Ed. Duane M. Searle (n.p.: n.p., 2012).
--------. "Shoulder Imbrued, The" (Henham). [Typescript with author's ms. corrections, 20 pgs.] New York Public Library.
--------. *Sleeping Waters* (Trevena). London: Constable and Co., 1913.
--------. *Tenebrae: A Novel* (Henham). London: Skeffington & Son, 1898.
--------. *Typet's Treasure* (Trevena). London: Chapman and Hall, 1927.
--------. "Under False Colours" (Henham). *Pearson's Magazine* 4:6 (December 1900): 659-666.
--------. *Under One Cover: Eleven Shories* (Henham *et. al.*). London: Skeffington & Son, 1898.
--------. *Vanished Moor, The* (Trevena). London: Mills and Boon, 1923.
--------. *Written in the Rain* (Trevena). London: Mills and Boon, 1910.
"Trevena's Cornish Story is Part Idyl and Part Melodrama," rev. of *Furze.Chicago Daily.* 6 June 1908: 9.
Tylor, E. B. *Primitive Culture.* 2 vols. London: John Murray,1871.

U - Z

Van Pelt, Cornelia. "Twelve Books of the Month VII," rev. of *Sleeping Waters. Bookman.* (March 1915): 99.

Ward, Mary Arnold, rev. of *Marius the Epicurean*, by W. Pater. *Macmillan's Magazine.* 52 (June 1885): 134.

Weygandt, Cornelius. *A Century of the English Novel.* New York: The Century Co., 1925.

Williams, Harold. *Modern English Writers.* New York: Alfred Knopf, 1919.

Woolf, Virginia. "Modern Fiction." *The Common Reader*, First Series. Hogarth Press: London, 1925: 184-193.

Wordsworth, William. *Poetical Works.* Ed. T. Hutchinson and E. deSelincourt. London: Oxford U.P., 1950.

Yeats, W.B. "J. M. Synge and Ireland." *Essays and Introductions.* London: Macmillan, 1961.

Young, Gordon Ray. "Literature and Art /Visions on Dartmoor," rev. of *Sleeping Waters. Los Angeles Times.*21 February 1915: Part IIIa.

Index

Zeitfracht Medien GmbH
Ferdinand-Jühlke-Straße 7
99095 Erfurt, Deutschland
produktsicherheit@kolibri360.de